THE RED MANDARINS

THE RED MANDARINS

Travels in Red China

by

KARL ESKELUND

TAPLINGER PUBLISHING CO., INC.
NEW YORK
1961

Copyright © Karl Eskelund 1959

Library of Congress Catalog Card No. 60-13010

First published in the United States by
TAPLINGER PUBLISHING CO., INC., 1961

PRINTED IN GREAT BRITAIN BY
BRISTOL TYPESETTING CO. LTD.
STOKES CROFT - BRISTOL

CONTENTS

ILLUSTRATIONS

Colour

In present-day China many people wear white masks against infection.

My mother-in-law's two housegirls—now called housekeepers.

The wandering plumber is still heard crying through the streets.

Old People's Home in Peking—some of the inmates enjoying the sunshine.

The correct way of eating rice—scoop it in with chopsticks!
Outdoor street restaurant in Peking.

What they grow on their "private" piece of ground the farmers are allowed to sell in the towns.

The spring festival is celebrated also in Communist China.

Fabulous dog on guard at the entrance of the temple.

The Bund in Shanghai—once the beating heart of the city.

Peasants bringing their wares to "the free market" in town.

Green vegetables being pitted for the winter—everything is now done collectively.

Street library—all books expressing the "incorrect" attitude have been confiscated.

In spite of all upheavals there is something unchangeable about China.

First and foremost it is the young that the Communists try to win over.

Sugar-coated hawthorn berries on a stick is a Chinese delicacy.

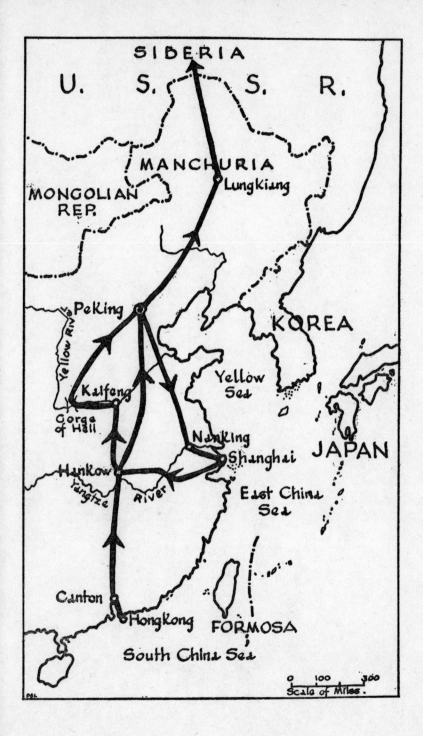

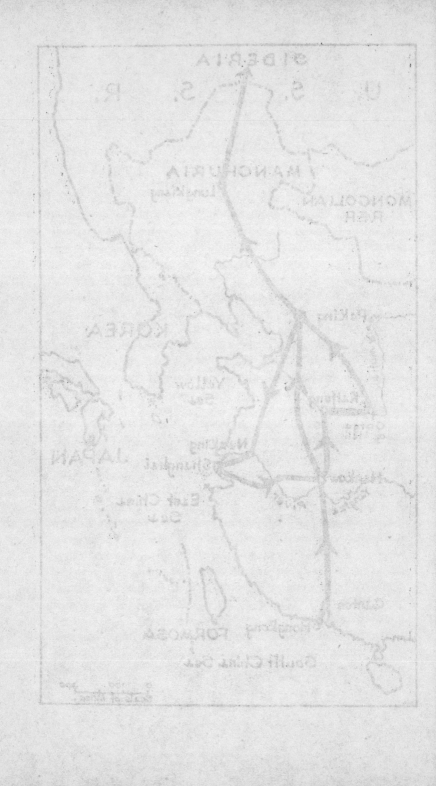

CHAPTER I

Home To Peking

IT WAS HARD to imagine that we were in the heart of a
city with as many inhabitants as all Denmark. The streets
were deserted although it was only nine o'clock in the evening.
The first snow of winter crunched underneath the wheels.
Otherwise one could only hear the heavy breathing of the
rickshawmen, and then of course my voice. I always chatter
away when excited.

The street lamps swung in the wind, lonely islands of light
in the dark night. The broad street was lined with one-storied
houses, but now a tremendous building loomed ahead. The
slanting roof, powdered with a fine layer of snow, stood out
clearly against the starlit sky. I jumped up—here was something I could recognize!

" It's the Gate of Heavenly Peace! Chi-yun, do you . . ." I
did not get any further. The light vehicle swayed perilously
from the sudden shifting of weight. My rickshawman turned
his head and looked reproachfully at me. I sat down again,
crestfallen, and tried to calm myself.

It wasn't easy. Memories rushed through my head. It was
here in Peking that Chi-yun and I first met. That was in 1936
when we were studying at the same university. How nervous
we were that day when she took me to her home and introduced me to her father, one of the leading businessmen in the
city. Our fears were well-founded. He gave us a long lecture
about filial piety, ending up by saying that he was against
mixed marriages.

The following year Chi-yun ran away from home and met
me in Shanghai, where we were married. Shortly after the
wedding we made a trip back to Peking. Her father had for-

11

given us and invited us home. The trip was like a honeymoon. Every day Chi-yun and I would go for long walks in the city where she was born and brought up; through her I came to know it and love it.

We had not been back to Peking since then, but we missed it. Often, when we could not fall asleep at night, we would lie and talk about it. We knew that the chance of seeing it again was slight, but that only increased its attraction. Red China was a closed country.

Then one day in the late summer of 1956 we got a telephone call from the Chinese Legation in Copenhagen. Several other Danish journalists had applied in vain for visas, but for some reason or other we had found favour in the eyes of the Chinese Communists. Maybe it was because we were slightly acquainted with Chou En-lai, or maybe because I had once punched Chiang Kai-shek's son on the jaw. Who knows?

And now we were here. After travelling for a month and a half, first through Europe and Asia Minor, on by ship via India and Indonesia to Hong Kong, and then by train through China from south to north, we had finally reached our goal. Just half an hour ago we had got off the train at Peking's tiny railroad station. Here we were stopped by a soldier who demanded to see our passports. He took off his heavy leather gloves and jotted down our names and passport numbers. We were told to report to the security police the following day . . .

I glanced at Chi-yun in the other rickshaw. After fifteen long years that had shaken China to its very foundation, she was back in her home town. In a few minutes she would see her mother again. But she sat with her hands in her lap, as calm and self-possessed as ever.

We drove through a tunnel-like city gate. It was nice no longer to be pulled by a man running between the shafts like a draught animal. In new China the rickshawman sits on a bicycle that pulls the vehicle.

Soon we came to a boulevard that ran along the wall surrounding the Forbidden City. In the darkness we would distinguish the outlines of the palaces where the emperors had once lived in secluded splendour. The Forbidden City, now a museum, lies in the centre of Peking. Surrounding it in a great square is the old city wall, and outside this again, almost seven miles from the centre of the city, is the outer wall. The imperial city was well protected—and yet it fell many times to the barbarians.

I began to wonder, as I had often done, why Peking never gives one a feeling of being in a big city. Perhaps it is because of the many parks and because the houses do not lie close together. Each home is surrounded by a wall. Only a few main streets are lined by unbroken rows of houses, but even here the buildings are no more than two storeys high. Until half a century ago it was forbidden to build higher than the imperial palaces, and inner Peking has changed little since then.

A drawn-out cry echoed in the night. It was a street pedlar with a basket hanging from each end of a pole carried on his shoulder. When he passed under a street light his breath looked like puffs of steam in the cold air. He repeated his call: "Turnips! Sweet as a pear, if too peppery I'll exchange them!" Chi-yun smiled. It was just like the old days. The northern Chinese don't eat much fruit in the winter, it is too expensive, but they get their vitamins from delicious raw turnips. Personally I prefer the golden Chinese persimmons, frozen like ice cream.

When we came to *Middle-section-of-the-elephant-trunk* lane, Chi-yun told me that here she had once attended kindergarten. She was brought here and fetched by the family's private rickshaw. Only when she grew bigger was she permitted to ride a bicycle.

I come from a three-room apartment in Copenhagen, so to me it always sounds like a fairy tale when my wife tells me about her childhood home. There were close to a hundred rooms, grouped around half a dozen courtyards. Only a few times in her life had Chi-yun entered the kitchen. It was in the back, close to the servants' quarters. Her grandparents had a courtyard to themselves. Grandfather had been a druggist in his younger days, but as soon as his son—Chi-yun's father—began to earn money, he stopped working. Everybody thought it quite natural that his son supported him ...

At *The street of the lantern-makers* the rickshawmen stopped in front of a large gate. The last time we came out of that gate we had been accompanied by Chi-yun's father. He had died shortly before the Communists came to power. Since then, Chi-yun's six sisters and brothers had left the childhood home; five of them had settled down outside China. We had heard from Chi-yun's mother a couple of times a year. The letters did not tell much; we knew practically nothing about how she had managed under the Communists.

Chi-yun went up to the gate and raised the door-knocker. It fell with a hollow clang.

" Who are you looking for ?"

" Mrs. Fei, the mistress of the house."

" No one by that name lives here."

" But that's impossible !" A note of desperation had crept into Chi-yun's voice. " For more than thirty years this has been the house of the Fei family. I was born here, Mrs. Fei is my mother . . ."

" Oh, now I know," the voice interrupted her. " You must mean Comrade Kang." Kang is Mrs. Fei's maiden name. Only later did we learn that nowadays women don't use their husband's names. It is considered old-fashioned—or feudal, as I have heard some Communists say. It turned out that Chi-yun's mother lived around the corner in a little house that was part of the property. We carried our suitcases to a smaller gate. Chi-yun looked about her in surprise.

" I think I have only been here a few times in my life—it was one of the side entrances to our home, we never used it. I used to think of it as a street. Now it is just a tiny alley."

Again she knocked. It seemed to me that several minutes passed before we heard steps.

" Who is it ?"

" It is I—Miss Fei."

" Which Miss Fei ?" The voice shook.

" The second daughter."

The door was unbolted and thrown open. In the dim light of the street lamp it was almost as if Chi-yun were standing there before me—only a little older and heavier. For a moment

mother and daughter looked at each other. Then they embraced. It was good to see that even Chinese can give way to
their feelings. They quickly collected themselves, though, and
dried away their tears.

" Chih fan la ma?" were Mrs. Fei's first words when we had
stamped the snow off our feet and entered the house. That is
an ancient greeting in China—have you eaten? Food comes
first in this country where people for so long have lived on the
edge of starvation

But Chi-yun first wanted answers to all the questions which
had accumulated since she left. What had happened to the
family property? How was life under the Communists? Had
she had a hard time?

" How long are you going to stay?" Mrs. Fei interrupted.
The last time I was here she had worn long silk dresses with
high collar. Now she had on thick, cotton-padded jacket and
trousers. It made her look round and clumsy. When she heard
that we had only a three-month visa she became so downcast
that Chi-yun went over and put her arm around her.

" You mustn't be sad about our leaving, Mother. After all,
we have just come."

Mrs. Fei tried to smile, but soon her face became worried
again. " Will it be all right for you to live here?"

We looked at her in surprise. Where else? After all, this
was Chi-yun's home . . .

" Please don't misunderstand me," she quickly added. She
would like so much to have us stay with her, but what would
the authorities say? There were certain hotels where foreign
visitors were supposed to stay. One must be careful not to do
the wrong thing.

" But we can't find out now. Tonight you stay here, then
we can inquire tomorrow morning. I'll make a bed for you in
the living-room . . ."

My wife looked about the little room. There were several
angular Chinese chairs of polished wood and a couple of carved
chests. They didn't go very well with the piano and the European sofa, I thought. There was far too much furniture, but
who has the heart to store away things that have come to mean

something to one? The desk was covered with pictures of Mrs. Fei's children and grandchildren—I quickly found one of my wife as a skinny little girl with a pair of steel-rimmed glasses perched on her snub nose.

"But this is grandfather's old room, isn't it?" Chi-yun exclaimed. "It used to be full of potted plants and bird cages." She had told me how the old man used to go for a walk in the park with one of his birds every morning. For hours he would chat with the other old men while the birds sang to each other. If a bird had a poor voice it wasn't allowed to join —it might have a bad influence on the others.

Mrs. Fei nodded. "Yes, your grandfather died shortly after your father died." A few years later she had sold the old home with the exception of this and three other small rooms and a tiny courtyard. The authorities had not confiscated anything from her; she did not belong to the category of enemies of the people or exploiters of the poor. She had bought government bonds with part of the money. She was managing very well— far better than most people. Many families now had to live in dormitories, for there was a housing shortage in Peking.

She went over and put her hand on a radiator. "I even have the luxury of central heating." And what on earth would she do with more than four rooms, now that she lived alone with her mother-in-law? The old lady would undoubtedly live until she became a hundred; she was already ninety-four, but could hardly recognize people any more. The only thing that really interested her was food—preferably sweet things. But she still knew how to complain, and of course it was the daughter-in-law who had to listen to her. It was not easy to take care of the old lady, but Mrs. Fei was fortunate in having two housekeepers . . .

"*Housekeepers?*" Chi-yun looked questioningly at her mother. Yes, one did not call them amahs or servants any more. That was undemocratic. Tonight they were both attending a meeting of the street committee . . .

We put two sofas together in the living-room which was also furnished in a mixed Chinese and European style. We were tired after the long journey and went to bed. When we

In present-day China many people wear white masks against infection.

My mother-in-law's two housegirls – now called housekeepers.

had turned off the light, Chi-yun and her mother went on talking through the open door. There was so much my wife wanted to know. What had become of Li-cheng whom she used to admire so much? And Yu-ling who went dancing with her—that was not very often, for Mr. Fei was strict with his daughters. And Pei-chen and Ming-deh . . .

The big families were now broken up and my wife's childhood friends were scattered. No one could afford to keep so many servants any more, and the old people had lost their authority over the young. Some of her friends were working for the government in distant provinces. Others had fled to Hong Kong or Formosa just before the Communists came. One had committed suicide—she could not adjust herself to the new way of life. Two had been in prison for several years, but as far as she knew they had been released.

" I know so little of what is going on," Mrs. Fei said. In the old days she was busy managing the big household. Now time passed slowly. During the summer she cultivated roses in her courtyard. She studied Russian through the radio; she already knew several hundred words . . .

The last time we were here—that was during the Japanese occupation—Mrs. Fei had studied Japanese over the radio.

" I don't see many people any more," she continued. " There is hardly any social life—people have neither the time nor the money. When they are not working they attend meetings."

" How are Mei-ling's parents?" Chi-yun asked. " Are they still in Peking?" They are. Mei-ling, Chi-yun's best friend, was now in the United States. She had written Chi-yun and asked her to look up her parents.

" Karl and I will pay them a visit tomorrow," Chi-yun said.

" They will be happy to see you and hear about Mei-ling," Mrs. Fei said, but did not sound convinced. " It will be better, though, to let them know beforehand that you are coming."

" Why, is that necessary?"

" I think it is wiser. They are old people, they get nervous very easily, and—later on you will understand. Many things have changed since you went away . . ."

That was the last thing I heard before I fell asleep.

B

CHAPTER II

The White Masks

WHEN I OPENED my eyes the next morning two women were looking at me. Mrs. Fei's two old maidservants were taken aback when the foreign son-in-law suddenly sat up in bed and nodded to them. But when I bade them good morning in their own language they smiled. If I spoke Chinese—even with a laughable accent—I could not be such a barbarian. *Erh Gu Yieh,* they called me—Second Daughter's Husband.

For breakfast we had noodles, which the Italians learned about from China through Marco Polo. In North China you always eat noodles when somebody has a birthday. They are a symbol of long life. Today was the thirty-seventh birthday of one of Chi-yun's brothers, now a professor at an American university.

After breakfast Mrs. Fei reminded us that we had to report to the police. " Be sure to obey the laws," she said. " If you do that, you will never have any troubles with the authorities."

She accompanied us part of the way. We were almost blinded when we opened the door. The city was covered by snow which muffled the sounds of the street and glittered in the sun. In the distance we could see the majestic towers of the city wall. These towers are ninety-nine feet high—if they were more, they would antagonize the evil spirits. In China, they always hover one hundred feet or more above the ground—or at least they did in the old days.

A scissors-grinder blew his long horn, and the housewives came out with the big chopping knives that you find in every Chinese kitchen. The man's grinding stone was fastened to a wooden bench which he carried on his shoulder; he set it down in the snow and went to work.

18

"How clean Peking has become!" Chi-yun exclaimed. When she was a child there was no public garbage collecting, so people often emptied their garbage pails in the street. No one would dream of doing that any more, her mother said. "The neighbours would protest. Since the Communists came we have learned to look differently at such things. In the old days most people didn't care how the city looked. Now we are proud of Peking."

A little boy squatted in the gutter and relieved himself. Like all Chinese babies, he wore pants that were slit in the back. "We have also tried to teach the children not to use the streets as a public toilet," Mrs. Fei remarked with a smile. "But we haven't succeeded yet."

An ox-cart came creaking by. The driver cracked his whip, but the lumbering animal kept its own slow pace. An icicle hung from its steaming muzzle. We laughed when we discovered that there was a small bag hanging under the ox's tail. Mrs. Fei told us that all the beasts of burden now have such a bag. In this way the streets are kept clean and no fertilizer is wasted.

The mangy dogs that used to roam the streets have also disappeared. A friend of mine, a foreign diplomat, later told me that when he goes walking with his dog, children surround him and discuss what kind of animal it is. A few years ago the Communists decided that dogs were a menace to public health and a burden to the national economy, so they were all exterminated.

From habit I looked right and left before we crossed a street. It really wasn't necessary. Though the population of Peking has increased from about one million to more than four since the Communists made it the capital, the traffic is as slow as before. There are blessedly few motor cars.

Nor are there as many rickshaws as before. The Communists consider this means of conveyance a shameful leftover from the capitalistic past, and few new ones are being made. The profession is to die out with the present generation of rickshaw-pullers.

The few motor cars that passed by were mainly of Russian

or Eastern European make. They had to move cautiously on the icy streets. There were many new buses, all from Skoda. Long queues waited at every bus stop, and once we heard angry shouts from a passenger who had got his arm caught in the door—he had only managed to get part of himself squeezed inside the crowded bus.

In the old days many people had been dressed in rags. Now it looked as if everybody had just got a new suit of clothes. All wore uniform-like outfits of blue cloth. The thick, cotton-padded suits hid the lines of the body so you could hardly tell the difference between men and women. Even Mrs. Fei looked like a soldier.

We saw many people with white masks over their mouths—they looked like surgeons or nurses who had just emerged from the operating theatre. Mrs. Fei explained that it had become a custom to wear such masks. She had one herself. They had been introduced by the Communists, for hygienic reasons. They protect against bacteria and against the dust which is a plague in North China both summer and winter. A few days later, when we attended a ball in the Workers' Palace, some of the dancers wore the white masks—it did not look very romantic.

There were queues outside some shops. It is often difficult to get certain foods, especially pork. Mrs. Fei was going shopping, so we left her at the entrance of the big market.

The security police had headquarters in an old palace close to the Forbidden City. We were asked about our plans and were told that if we wanted to travel outside the capital, we had to ask for permission three days ahead. As soon as we came to a new town we would have to report our arrival to the police.

On our way home we visited Mei-ling's parents. At the entrance to the compound where they lived we had to write down our names and address. In the old days Mei-ling's father had been a wealthy man, but now the old couple lived in one room. Here too there was too much furniture. As soon as we saw Mei-ling's parents we regretted that we had not followed Mrs. Fei's advice and informed them that we were coming.

Even before we had sat down, Mei-ling's father asked whether we had given our names to the gateman. And had we written them down in English? We nodded. Why was he worried about that? He murmured something about my being a foreigner and then changed the subject. Only now did they remember to offer us tea—not freshly-made tea like in the old days, but a dark essence diluted with hot water.

" We have no servants any more," Mei-ling's mother said apologetically. " We live very simply."

" We are getting along quite well," her husband quickly added. " We are satisfied, we have nothing to complain about."

The old man smoked continuously; his long fingers were stained with nicotine. We told them what we knew about Mei-ling. When we said goodbye we had a feeling that they were relieved. That was strange, for in the old days Mei-ling's father had been especially fond of my wife.

When we came out, a whistling in the air made us look up. A flock of pigeons came swooping above the slanting roofs of the city. The leader of the flock has a whistle tied to its leg, Chi-yun told me. Sometimes the sound attracts other pigeons to join the flock. It used to be a sport to increase your number of pigeons in this way, but there are not many who keep them any more. It is difficult to get fodder for them.

We came to a large, new building. It was a strange mixture —the building itself had Chinese lines and decorative columns, but the flat roof was strictly functional. It made me think of a man in evening clothes with a cap on his head.

A few days later we got the explanation. The architect had tried to make the building fit its surroundings, but just before it was completed the government started a campaign against waste. The architect did not escape unscathed. Indignant editorials pointed to the pillars as an example of extravagance and misuse of public funds. The poor architect had to confess publicly that he was guilty of " bourgeoisie-idealistic divergencies." He could not very well have the columns torn down, but as penance he crowned the building with a flat roof . . .

A pleasant surprise awaited us when we came home. Mrs. Fei had sent for Chi-yun's eldest sister, Chiao-yun. She is the only one of the Fei children who is still living in China. The two sisters embraced without a word.

" And here are my children." Chiao-yun pointed at two tall boys and a ten-year-old girl wearing big horn-rimmed glasses. " I have one more at home, but she is still a baby, so I couldn't bring her."

We showed them pictures of Mei-mei, our daughter Why hadn't we brought her along? And why did we have only one child? Here Mrs. Fei looked reproachfully at me. We had no son . . .

The door was suddenly opened and the servant showed in a man in blue uniform. He greeted us politely and sat down. Twice he refused before he accepted a cup of tea. When we had talked for a while about the unusually early winter he congratulated Comrade Kang because her daughter and son-in-law had come to visit her. He hoped we would get a good impression of the new, democratic China. How long were we going to stay and what were our plans? We answered his questions in the same light conversational tone. How nice it was that we could stay at home with Comrade Kang instead of living at a hotel, he finally said . . .

Mrs. Fei smiled happily. When the policeman left she remarked that he was an unusually nice young man, always so polite. He paid her a visit every once in a while. How different from the old days, when everybody was afraid of the police . . .

Chiao-yun had brought along a fur coat which she handed my wife. " It is for you," she said. " Father gave it to me just before he died. It has been hanging in the closet ever since."

It fitted Chi-yun beautifully. Gently she stroked the soft fur which reeked of mothballs.

" No, you keep it," Chi-yun protested. " The winters are much colder here than in Denmark—I don't want to take it away from you."

" But I have no use for it. Nobody wears a fur coat any more."

" Why not?"

Her sister shrugged. " It would look strange. Of course there is no law against it, but—but everybody would stare at you. People are all dressed alike now, haven't you noticed?"

"Yes, and nobody uses make-up any more, not even lipstick," Chi-yun said. Chinese woman have used cosmetics since the time of Confucius. "And before, all the girls used to curl their hair—now nobody does."

Chiao-yun explained that everybody wants to be like the Communists who scorn such frivolities. But during the last few months the newspapers had been encouraging the women to use make-up and dress more attractively—I guess the authorities realized that the uniformity had a depressing effect. Hardly any had followed the government's suggestion, however. People were afraid of being different.

Chi-yun thanked her sister for the fine present. Chiao-yun told us that she was going to start working at a children's hospital the very next day. She was a nurse, but when she married and began to have children she had given up her profession in order to devote all her time to her family. Her husband, Ai-teh, was a doctor. We asked her why she wanted to start working again. Was it because Ai-teh did not make enough money?

No, they managed quite well, even though doctors did not make as much as before. Nobody had private practice any more, all doctors were employed by the government. But there was a shortage of nurses, and people thought it was wrong of her not to help out. Everybody worked nowadays. She wasn't especially eager to start again because of the new baby, but she wanted to do her duty . . .

Her eldest son nodded approvingly. He was nearly sixteen and belonged to the Communist Youth League, which has more than twenty million members. I asked if he intended to join the Communist party when he was old enough.

Yes, if they would accept him, he answered. Most young people wanted to, but it was not so easy. You had to have self-discipline, to be ready to sacrifice everything for your country, otherwise you were not eligible.

Mrs. Fei and Chiao-yun wanted to hear about our journey from Europe. The young fellow did not seem very interested when we described the countries we had visited. He asked if we had been to any of the People's Democracies. When Chi-yun nodded his face brightened.

" We were in Yugoslavia."

Oh, Yugoslavia—but they were not real Communists there. Chi-yun now began telling them about Scandinavia. Before long her nephew broke in with a question. How was it possible that people were so well off in northern Europe? After all, those were capitalist countries, and in capitalist countries the people were oppressed and exploited by the upper classes . . .

I was about to set him straight, when Chi-yun looked at me. I could tell that she did not want me to say anything.

" Do you think that the Russians are better off than the Scandinavians?" I asked the boy.

" Of course. The Soviet Union is the most delevoped country in the world, it has the highest standard of living."

Chiao-yun must have known better, but she did not say anything. I understood her. What was the use of telling him something that was different from what all the other young people were learning? It would only bewilder him, and it might be dangerous . . .

We accompanied Chiao-yun and her children to the gate. The afternoon sun shone warmly, the snow had begun to melt, but it was cold in the shade. When we waved goodbye to them I thought of what Mrs. Fei had said the previous evening. She was right. Many things had changed in China.

CHAPTER III

A Question Of Time

I WILL NEVER forget an experience I had many years ago. I had not been long in China then. Perhaps that is why it made such a strong impression on me. I was fresh from Denmark, not yet used to the poverty and suffering of the East.

It was a bitterly cold winter evening in Peking. I was on my way to visit some Danish friends, when I saw a man struck by a hit-and-run driver. A crowd gathered around the unconscious man who had a bleeding wound in the temple. A policeman dragged him up on the sidewalk and was about to walk away, when I grabbed him by the arm.

"But you can't leave him here—you must get him to a hospital!"

The policeman looked at the wounded man. It was an old farmer, probably a refugee from a famine district. I suppose he had come to the city to beg. His cotton gown was worn and patched.

"It costs money to stay at the hospital," the policeman explained kindly. "He can't get in without someone to guarantee for him. Most likely he has no relatives here in town. Who is going to help a stranger?"

I don't think the Chinese are more callous than people in other countries, but there was no public welfare in the old days. People only felt responsible for members of their own clan . . .

I didn't even have any money on me, so what could I do? When I arrived at my friends' home, distressed by what I had seen, they tried to comfort me. We were foreigners. It wasn't our fault that there was so much misery in China. There was nothing we could do—the problem was so hopelessly big.

25

Later in the evening, when I returned by the same road, the old man was no longer there. Only a pool of frozen blood remained on the spot where he had been lying . . .

Now, twenty years later, my wife and I came walking down the same street. It was early in December and the sun was shining from a clear blue sky—it does practically all year round in Peking. We were on our way to visit two places—an old-age-home and a prison.

Just as we were going to cross the street I saw an old man leaning against a wall. He has had too much to drink, was my first thought, but that was so unlikely. During all my years in China I have never seen a drunken Chinese.

We took another look at the old man and saw that tears were running down his face. Some people stopped and began to question him. Why was he weeping? He explained that he was from a village sixty miles away. He had come to the city to sell peanuts and had lost his earnings, and now he didn't know how he could get home—he was an old man, it was too far to walk.

In the old days I would have suspected him of being a beggar playing a trick. At that time all the citizens of China were infested with starving wretches who exhibited their open sores or a sick child, or just stood with blind eyes, holding out a bowl. One tried to pretend that they weren't there and told oneself that they were probably professionals who didn't want to work for a living—people even said that the sick babies they carried had been rented . . .

One of the bystanders asked the old man how much a train ticket would cost. A little over one Yuan (about three shillings), the old man replied. Someone took out a ten-cent note—coins are no longer used in China. Someone else gave twenty cents, a third only five, but it quickly added up to more than a dollar. The old man smiled happily, bowing right and left, and hurried off to the railroad station.

" Imagine that this could happen in China!" Chi-yun said. " By the way, have you noticed that there are no beggars any more?"

I had—and not alone that. A couple of days ago I had given

twenty cents to a shoeshine boy who looked as if he needed a
meal. As I walked on he came running after me.

"I haven't shined your shoes," he said.

"They don't need it."

"Then I don't want your money—I am no beggar!"

Finally I had to stay and let him shine my shoes although
I had just polished them at home . . .

The street went past one of the small lakes which former
emperors had made in order to beautify Peking. Laughter
from some skating children rang in the frosty, clear air.
Through the melting snow you could see the tiles on the roofs
of the Forbidden City. They were golden yellow—the imperial
colour.

Some men were cutting out great blocks of ice. These are
kept in undergrown caverns and sold during the hot summer
months, Chi-yun told me. The Chinese have done this for more
than a thousand years.

Here on the outskirts of the city there were not so many
political placards on the walls. All year round the cities of
Red China are plastered with coloured posters that look like
enlarged comics. All the enemies of the people are hauled
over the coals—imperialists are speared by the bayonets of the
peoples' democracies, Dulles is blown up by his own atom
bombs, evil reactionaries, hands tied behind their backs, are
led away by noble-looking Red soldiers.

For a time Chiang Kai-shek was frequently under attack, but
when we came to Peking the slogans for the liberation of
Formosa had disappeared. Now Suez was in the limelight. It
seems that the Communists try to direct the hatred of the
people against one thing at a time.

Even so the people can't always keep pace with the changes.
Just before we came to China there was a monster rally in
Peking. Half a million people marched to the British Legation
to demonstrate against the attack on Suez—"a spontaneous
outburst of the people's indignation," the Chinese papers
called it.

A foreigner I know who speaks fluent Chinese was there
during the demonstration. He stopped a farm lad who was

carrying a placard with a picture of Nasser. Why was he demonstrating?

" For the liberation of Formosa," came the answer.

We stopped in front of a restaurant, a low, attractive stone building. Just outside the entrance, a young waiter was stirring something steaming in a tremendous iron pot. That'll make a good picture, I thought, but before I had finished adjusting the camera, the waiter gave a shout. He did not want to be photographed.

" Why not?"

" Who are you? Why do you want a picture of me?"

I showed him my fine red press card which had been issued by the Chinese Ministry of Foreign Affairs. It passed from hand to hand, for of course a crowd had gathered around us. Most of them were impressed. If the government had given me such a card I must be a friend of China, so it was probably all right for me to take the picture ...

In the old days, the waiter would undoubtedly have given in at this point. When two Chinese disagreed about something, the decision was often left to the bystanders. But the young man had grown up in new China and was not so easily swayed. Even if I was a journalist, it was by no means certain that I had permission to take pictures. He phoned the police. They referred him to the Ministry of Foreign Affairs. He had to give his name, age and address. When he had explained the case in detail, they asked him what he was cooking in the pot.

" Porridge," he replied. Some of the bystanders smiled discreetly, but the waiter kept his serious mien. A moment later the foreign ministry announced its decision. I was permitted to take the picture.

Close to the restaurant we came to a square that was swarming with people. Here was a " free market," as it is called. Buying and selling is otherwise controlled by the authorities, and the farmers are members of collectives which have to sell their produce to the government.

This arrangement caused such dissatisfaction that it threatened to affect the agricultural output. As soon as the government realized this is loosened the controls. Each farmer was permitted to cultivate a tiny plot of land for himself. What he produces here, he is allowed to take to the city and sell on the " free market." His prices are higher than those in the stores, but then the stores are often short of certain products which the farmers can supply.

The farmers at the market grinned when I photographed them. They have not yet been made " politically conscious "— an expression which the Communists often use. Therefore they do not realize that as a good Communist and patriotic Chinese —the two are practically synonymous today—you must always be on guard against " imperialistic enemies " and " reactionary elements."

We finally reached the old-age home, a group of one-storied houses surrounded by a wall. We were welcomed by the director, a former officer of China's Red Army. Tea was poured for us in the meeting hall under the usual portraits of Mao Tse-tung and Stalin. Destalinization never really reached China.

We asked the director if the government planned to take care of all old people. Oh no, that was still the duty of the family—the state only helped those who were alone and destitute.

In Peking there were two other homes like this one, each with about a thousand inmates, he told us. The place was originally used for the rehabilitation of beggars. Some of them had been so decrepit that it was useless to teach them a trade. They were still here. It cost the government a little under twenty pounds a year to care for each inmate. They were also provided with clothing and tobacco.

We would have preferred to wander around unescorted and talk to the old people, but the director wanted to take care of his foreign guests. When we came inside one of the dormitories where the old people lived, he gave an order. They all rose and clapped. Visitors are always greeted this way in new China. It is a custom which the Chinese have learned from the Soviet Union.

There was no doubt that the old people were happy to be there. " We get enough to eat," said an old man, who sat close to the stove, stroking his white beard. "And when we die, we will get a coffin and a proper funeral . . ."

My thoughts wandered back to a crooked alley in Shanghai during the old days. Here a Chinese charity organization had its headquarters—"The Blue Heaven Benevolent Funeral Association," I think it was called. On the sidewalk outside lay rows of dying beggars. Day and night, winter and summer they lay there, waiting to die and be buried in a coffin of rough boards—corpses picked up by the police were burned, a thought which the Chinese abhorred . . .

Some of the old people were sticking labels on matchboxes. It was nice to earn a little pocket money. Others sat on their beds, playing chess, or strolled outside keeping their hands folded together in their long sleeves. Gloves aren't used much in this country.

When we left, the old people applauded again. We went on to the prison. Two soldiers guarded the gate, but once we had passed them we did not have the feeling of being inside a prison. There were no guards, no locks on the doors. The prisoners were allowed to dress as they wanted. They were about the only people we saw in China who did not wear the uniform-like blue outfits.

The prison had a cotton spinnery where the inmates worked for eight and a half hours—the usual workday in China is only seven and a half hours. They got twenty per cent less pay than workers outside. They had to pay for their own food and were allowed to keep what was left over.

The prisoners had a dramatic society, an orchestra, and a football team. They exercised three times a day, twenty minutes each time. After work they had an hour of newspaper reading and discussion, followed by two hours of political education.

We were allowed to question anyone we wanted, said the warden, but when we faced the prisoners we found it hard to say anything. I have seldom felt as uncomfortable as I did in front of these silent men who avoided our eyes.

What had they done? I asked as we walked on. The warden replied that two-thirds of the prisoners had committed political offences. I looked at him in surprise. He explained that some of them had been agents of the Chiang Kai-shek régime. Others had been guilty of anti-revolutionary activities. They had a hostile attitude towards the changes introduced by the new government.

The prisoners are not addressed as *comrade,* the warden replied in answer to my query, " but we neither consider nor treat them as criminals. To us they are human beings who have been led astray."

He added that man is a product of his environment. The " incorrect attitude " of these people was a natural result of the bad influence of the old society. Here in the prison, they were given a chance to improve themselves. They were released as soon as they had changed their attitude. They only had to show that the political education had brought results—that they realized that the Communist programme was the only right thing for China.

" And if they are not convinced ?"

The warden smiled. " They are always convinced sooner or later. It is only a question of time."

It was getting dark when we came out into the street. A sharp wind blew from the north. It was very cold.

CHAPTER IV

My Wife Eats With Chopsticks

ONE DAY CHI-YUN and I were invited out for dinner by some European friends. We were to be there at seven-thirty, but around six o'clock that evening the maids at my mother-in-law's home began to set the table.

" I hope you haven't prepared anything for us," I said.

" We have," replied Chang-sao, the older one.

" But we're going out for dinner—we told you so."

" I know, but you are going to have western food." She discreetly avoided my eyes. " We thought that you had better eat something first."

Her opinion of European food is not uncommon among the Chinese. It is therefore surprising that the Soviet restaurant which was opened in Peking shortly after the liberation is rather well attended. The reason for this is political rather than culinary, however. Russia being the fatherland of socialism, some Chinese feel it a duty to try Russian food. At the Soviet restaurant, you can see them struggle bravely with the heavy, unimaginative food. Many give up halfway and never come back—the exception being a few fanatical Communists. " They don't let facts interfere with their theories," a Chinese friend told me jokingly. " Everything that comes from the U.S.S.R. *must* be the best—and that's that."

Of course I wanted my wife to get a good impression of Denmark the first time we went there together, so one of the first things I did was to take her to a famous Copenhagen restaurant and order a beefsteak for her. For years I had been telling her about the unsurpassed delights of the Danish kitchen. Now I watched her expectantly as she began eating— but no cries of joy escaped her lips. She just sat and chewed.

The wandering plumber is still heard crying through the streets.

Old People's Home in Peking – some of the inmates enjoying the sunshine.

" Is it tough?"

" Not at all."

" Do you like it?"

" One gets very big helpings in Denmark."

" But does it taste good?"

" I've never had such a big piece of meat before!"

I put down my knife and fork. " You know very well that I hate this beating about the bush. Give me a straight answer—do you like it or don't you?"

She smiled politely. " You are a very good writer. Sometimes your descriptions are better than the real thing."

For once I did not appreciate her compliment. I was deeply hurt. We Danes take our food seriously. If she had torn down the Danish flag and trampled on it, it could not have been worse.

" Do the Danes eat nothing but meat and potatoes?" she asked when we had chewed for a while in icy silence. I ordered a portion of vegetables for her. It looked delicious—steaming leeks, carrots and brussels sprouts—but after a couple of mouthfuls she pushed it over to me.

" *Now* what's the matter?"

" Nothing—I just don't feel like any."

" Why not?"

" Because . . ." She looked unhappily at me. " Because vegetables should be crisp!" it burst out of her. " They should be braised in a little oil, the way we do in China—but these have been boiled to death, they are like porridge in the mouth, they have no taste!"

I drew a deep breath. Then I played my last trump. I called the waiter and asked for the sandwich list. This restaurant was famous for having the longest list in all Denmark.

" What a choice!" I said, handing it to her. " Have you ever seen anything like it?"

She had. As politely as possible she reminded me that each province in China has a far bigger choice than one found on this list. There are eighteen provinces in China, not including Manchuria.

Even an open Danish sandwich of roast beef topped with

c

remoulade and crisp onions, and one with liverpaste decorated with meat jelly and slices of beetroot, failed to impress her. I have since discovered that hardly any Chinese appreciate our sandwiches. They look nice, they say, but are too dry.

Chi-yun has never learned to cook, but after being in Denmark for a while she began experimenting with Chinese food. She burned herself and the food, cut her fingers and had many other bitter experiences, but she persisted. It was self-defence.

My first acquaintance with Chinese food goes back to a funeral feast in a town near Shanghai. I was the only foreigner among more than a hundred guests, and when the meal was about to start we were shown into a large hall with a dozen large, round tables. But instead of sitting down, the guests began pulling at each other and bowing and scraping. None of them seemed to want to sit at the table opposite the door. I was hungry, so when they asked me to sit down there I immediately acquiesced. The others seemed a little surprised.

Only one of the guests spoke a little English, so he was put next to me. He explained that it is customary to refuse at least twice when you are asked to sit at this table. The first time the offer is a matter of courtesy. When repeated, it is a special courtesy, and the third time it is really meant. This table is reserved for the most important guests.

"And the guest of honour sits here, facing the door," he said with a smile, indicating my chair.

I still feel sad when I think of all that I missed at this meal. First we had twelve cold dishes: sea-slug sauté, smoked chicken and duck, crab meat in wine sauce, marinated mussels and many other exotic things. All the food was cut in small pieces and could thus be easily handled with chopsticks. Each time someone at our table found a choice morsel he would place it in my bowl. They could not talk to me—I had not learned Chinese as yet—but this was their way of being kind to the foreign guest.

"Don't eat too much now," my neighbour advised, but I did not listen. It tasted so good—especially the *century-old-eggs,* as we Europeans call them. They are made from ducks' eggs and are really not more than a few months old. You preserve them in a mixture of lime and clay. The egg-white turns dark brown, the yoke almost black, and they taste like ripe Camembert, only better.

After the cold food, the waiters began carrying in hot courses —sweet and sour pork ribs, shrimps in bamboo shoots, crisp Mandarin fish, curried chicken. Curry is a foreign dish in China.

My interpreter told me what every dish consisted of. One of them caused him a little trouble, but I finally learned that it was stewed testicles of squid.

When the meal had lasted for about an hour I began to wonder why nobody burped. To do so was good manners among the Chinese, I had heard—it showed that you appreciated the food. Could it be that they were waiting for me to start? After all, I had the seat of honour . . .

I used to be one of the best burpers in my class, and now I proved that I had not forgotten how to do it. Then I looked about me for approval, but there was only a moment of surprised silence. Later I found out that it is all right if you happen to burp at a Chinese feast, but you should do it discreetly and it is certainly not obligatory.

When a whole duck was served—it was so tender that it almost fell apart at the touch of the chopsticks—I sat back in my chair. "I can't get down another bite," I declared. My neighbour looked at me in consternation.

"But we have just started—the best dishes are coming!"

The others, wiser than I, had taken only a mouthful or two of each dish, so they could continue until course number sixty-four was carried in. Rice and *chicken-feet-ducks'-tongue-soup* ended the meal, and then fruit was served.

But this I remember only vaguely, for when I could not eat any more I had started drinking. Hot, yellow rice wine was served; it tasted somewhat like sherry. You could also get Chinese firewater, more potent than our Danish *snaps*. If you dip a finger in it, draw a line and apply a match, the flame leaps across the table. There was yet another kind of firewater which first made me wonder whether I was seeing things.

" Tell me, isn't there a lizard in that bottle?" I asked my neighbour.

" Yes, there is supposed to be. It improves the taste."

The Chinese drink practically only at feasts and then with restraint. When rice is served at the end of the meal, the drinking stops. The wine cups are tiny. Fingergames are sometimes played, with two participating at a time. The players thrust out the right hand, holding out a number of fingers. At the same time, both shout a number between one and ten. The one who guesses the total number of fingers held out by the two players is the winner.

I played with my neighbour and won the first round. Triumphantly I emptied my wine cup. Then I discovered that some of the others were choking back their laughter.

" In China it is the loser who drinks," my neighbour explained. He raised his cup. " *Gan-bei.*" That means *dry cup* and is the Chinese way of saying " bottoms up." From then on I did not try very hard to win.

It is expensive to eat well in Europe, but nothing compared to the cost of a really luxurious Chinese meal. In Hong Kong, where many rich Chinese refugees live, the newspapers recently wrote about a banquet for twelve persons that cost £480. Only the choicest of choice dishes are served on such occasions —bear's paw, swallow's nest soup, snake and kildcat. The southern Chinese are said to be fond of eating the brain of a live monkey. The poor animal's head is put through a hole in the centre of a table especially made for this purpose. The hair is removed with boiling water, and the skull is then cracked like a soft-boiled egg. I have never been able to confirm this story.

Snakes are a popular dish in hot, humid South China. In the big towns you find shops which sell nothing else. Chi-yun and I visited such a snake shop in Hong Kong. The owner told us that he sold about 10,000 snakes a day. They cost slightly less than one pound sterling apiece. The flesh is stewed or roasted, but the most sought-after titbit is the gall which you drink in a glass of wine. We tried a " cocktail " made up of the gall of five different snakes. I did not care very much for the bitter taste, but it is said to be good for the eyes.

In the old days the Chinese tipped liberally, and at parties in private homes the servants always got something from the guests. It was also customary for the host to tip the rickshaw-men waiting outside for their masters. As you were leaving a restaurant, the waiter would call out how much you had tipped, whereupon the other waiters chorused a loud " many thanks!" In this way you paid generously to avoid losing face. I have always disliked the tipping system and was happy to find that it had been banned in new China.

Only at feasts do the Chinese eat so much meat. Less than three per cent of their food consist of meat or fish, compared for instance to forty per cent in the U.S.A. The Chinese cannot afford to feed animals and then eat them—they eat the grain directly instead. The pigs that are kept by many farmers sub-sist mainly on refuse. They are black, and strangely enough they have no trichina.

The daily fare of the Chinese is very plain, consisting mainly of grain and vegetables. In the south, people eat rice three times a day; the northerners eat mainly noodles of bread made of corn or wheat.

A bottle of soya sauce takes the place of the salt cellar in a Chinese household. Milk and butter are never used. The food is fried in vegetable oil, preferably over a coal or charcoal fire. A foreigner in Hong Kong once told me that he had wanted to make life easier for his faithful old cook, so he bought an electric kitchen range. The next day he found his cook in the yard, preparing dinner over the old charcoal burner. " Only proper fire make proper food," he told his master.

The Chinese may not talk quite as much about food as we do in Denmark, but they are certainly no less interested in it. When you hear people complain in Red China, it is usually because of the shortage of food. Worst of all is the scarcity of cooking oil, caused by the export of peanuts. Soya beans and pork are also exported to the Soviet Union on a large scale as payment for machines. People realize that this is why they have to tighten their belts. There is some bitterness in the anecdote which they tell about the clever Soviet scientists who crossed a cow and a giraffe. The result was a strange animal with large udder and a very long neck.

"What do you suppose they use these animals for?" people ask. "To place along the Chinese border—they graze in China and are milked in Russia."

CHAPTER V

Confucius Returns

WHEN I WOKE up, I lay wondering for a moment. What was it I was looking forward to? Then I remembered where we were going today. I shook my wife, but she merely grunted and turned her back to me.

" Chi-yun," I said, " we're going to Yenching!"

That worked. A moment later she was out of bed, sweet and smiling, and I even got a good morning kiss. Yenching is our old university. It was here we first met, and just the name brought back memories of the time when we were eighteen and in love.

" Don't forget to put on your woollen underpants, Chi-yun," came Mrs. Fei's voice from the next room. She still treated her daughter as if she were a child. I was not excluded from her motherly solicitude, either. When we were about to leave, she came running with a woollen scarf. I had better tie it over my head, she said—the wind was very cold and I had no hat.

I assured her that it was quite unnecessary. I would turn up my collar, I never caught colds . . . I did not quite succeed in convincing her, but at least I escaped from being dressed up like an old farm woman.

Half an hour later Chi-yun and I drove out through the Western City Gate. For a moment I thought that we were on the wrong bus. I knew the road so well from the old days—this was where the city stopped and one was suddenly in the country. But all the little farmhouses with paper windows had disappeared, and where there once were fields was now one great building complex after the other.

They must be factories, I thought. The air was full of smoke and the place had the impersonal atmosphere of an industrial district. But for the characters above the gateways, one would not have thought that this was China. Chi-yun translated them for me.

Geological Institute, School of Metallurgy, School of Mining, Department of Chemistry . . .

And so it went on. A whole town had mushroomed since the Communists came into power in 1949, and it was still growing. Scaffolds reached towards the sky, horsecarts came rumbling, loaded with bricks.

It was refreshing finally to see old Yenching which is one of the most beautiful universities in the world. Chinese-style buildings are scattered over a large campus among artificial lakes and hills and a lovely pagoda. The sunlight sparkled on the glazed tiles of the slanting roofs as if to bid us welcome home.

We got out of the bus and walked towards the entrance. I took Chi-yun's hand. Do you remember . . . Over there was the library where I had sat at the same table evening after evening, well groomed and in my best suit. I don't think I ever finished a page—I was too busy gazing at a Chinese girl who blushed and pretended not to see me. And beyond, underneath a big tree by the tennis court, was the bench where I had kissed her the first time . . .

" Hey—where are you going?" A uniformed man beckoned us back to the gate. In the old days we had entered and left as we pleased, but now we first had to telephone Mr. Liang with whom we had an appointment. We did not know him; the meeting had been arranged by the foreign office. We filled a printed form with our names and address and the gateman stamped it.

" Remember to have Comrade Liang sign it," he called after us. " Otherwise you cannot get out."

Mr. Liang, a plump youngish man who was secretary to the president of the university, received us in a small meeting hall. In Red China, all contact between people seems to take place in meeting halls. As soon as I saw Mr. Liang, I began a guessing game which I have become addicted to since our arrival in this country. I try to figure out whether or not people belong to the Communist party.

Liang seemed to possess all the characteristics of a Chinese Communist. He was kind, understanding, straightforward, but his smiles and movements seemed deliberate. There was a slight touch of condescension in his manner, and he seemed to lack the usual sense of humour of the Chinese. He was very sure of himself, one felt that no sudden impulses were ever permitted to disturb his composure. It was the head that ruled, not the heart.

" Are you a member of the Communist party ?"

He looked at me and nodded. Opposite us sat a bespectacled young man with notebook and pencil held in readiness. That was Mr. Liang's secretary who was going to take down our conversation. The mere sight of him took away my desire to make the interview. Now I understood why some people suddenly become dumbstruck when I take out my notebook.

" How many students are there at the university ?"

Mr. Liang handed each of us a mimeographed sheet, filled with statistics about new China's progress in the field of higher education. It was impressive. Since the liberation—that is to say : since the Communists came to power—Yenching had been merged with two other universities. The number of students had increased from barely 800 to 8011. 21.5 per cent of them were girls, 22 per cent came from worker or peasant families. There were also 310 students from the Soviet Union and the other Peoples' Democracies. In Peking alone there were twenty-one new colleges and universities, and in all China, 217,000 youths had graduated from higher institutions of learning since 1949. That was 7,000 more than during the previous fifty years . . .

I got up and thanked Mr. Liang. Here was all the factual information I needed. Now we would like to talk to some students, but we could manage that ourselves—we knew the place so well.

Oh, no, Mr. Liang would not hear of that. It was his duty to help foreign guests, he said. He told his secretary to make some telephone calls. A while later six students came, two of them girls.

It was as if twenty years suddenly vanished. These students could easily have been my old schoolmates. They had the same intense earnestness that made them seem older than European students of the same age. Then suddenly they would start laughing and giggling over nothing. How childish, one thought, until one realized that it was shyness. They felt unsure of themselves, especially in the company of foreigners. Perhaps it was partly because they had been brought up under the Chinese family system. They had been taught to obey, not to think and act independently.

But when Chi-yun and I had talked for a while with the six students, we discovered that there was a difference after all. The first thing they asked me was what I thought of new China. I replied that there were many improvements since I had been here last. The distribution of wealth was more equal than before. Those who belonged to the former lower classes were no longer cringing and humble. They had acquired self-confidence. The amount of building done since 1949 was fantastic . . .

I kept waiting for them to contradict me. Common courtesy almost required them to do so—when you praise the food in China, the host must answer that it is poor fare, not fit to be served to guests. But these young people nodded and smiled— and then they even begun to outdo me in praising their own country!

Chi-yun and I soon discovered that they kept repeating certain words and phrases. Now Chinese students have always had a tendency to learn by heart. I suppose it is because they have to start memorizing the many Chinese characters from early childhood. Their memory is highly developed, but not their ability to judge. When during my student days I had discussions with my Chinese schoolmates, I would often catch them reeling off something which they did not understand. They had just learned it by heart from some book.

But in those days they had at least memorized whatever they pleased. Now they could hardly say anything without quoting

Marx or Lenin or Chairman Mao, as he is called in China. If one student got stuck, another one would quickly complete the quotation for him. And when one of them said something, the others would nod approvingly. That was almost the worst part of it—they did not seem to disagree about anything.

I could tell that Chi-yun was also disappointed to find the students so one-track minded. We had no feeling of contact with them. I soon got a suspicion, though, that the marxistic phrases which they kept reciting did not mean very much to them. Sometimes they did not even seem to understand them. But they could clearly see the progress which China had made under the Communists. *That* meant a great deal to them.

"I'm going to be an engineer," said Wu, a stocky fellow who bit his lips when he became excited. "What opportunity would I have had if I had lived under the reactionary Kuomintang régime? I could have taught other Chinese students who, like me, would never get a chance to practise what they learned. Or I could have got a minor position in a foreign engineering firm. At that time, the foreigners were in charge of all important engineering projects in China. Chinese were never given important posts. The foreigners looked down on us.

"It isn't like that in new China. We're respected now. We build our own bridges and dams and power plants. We're even beginning to make motor cars and airplanes . . ."

One of the girls broke in. She had a habit of emphasizing her words with sudden nods that sent her plaits flying. When the Communists entered the large cities along the coast, there were many girls in the Red Army. They all wore their hair in two long plaits, like farm girls, and since then it has been the fashion.

"I'm going to be a journalist," she said. "What chance would I have had when the reactionary Chiang Kai-shek clique was in power? A journalist couldn't get anywhere except by writing lying, reactionary propaganda . . ."

"Don't Chinese journalists write propaganda today?"

"Yes, but that's *true* propaganda!" The plaits flew. "It is our duty to make the people join the struggle against reactior ary enemies inside the country and imperialistic enemies outside. We must make the people realize how grateful we all should be because Chairman Mao and the Communist party have united our country and made it strong and respected . . ."

The others nodded eagerly. I thought of the anti-Japanese demonstrations that had often taken place when I was a student here. Then the students' feelings had also run high, but in general they had been disillusioned and apprehensive about the future. In those days China was corrupt and torn by civil war. The students had no respect for the government. They longed to do something for their country, but how could they? As the girl had said : in those days you got nowhere except by licking the boots of those in power.

" In new China there is no corruption," she concluded. " All the people work together towards a common goal."

" Yes, there certainly is a new spirit," I said. " In many ways the Communists are idealists . . ."

" No!" they all protested. Chi-yun and I looked at them in surprise.

" Idealism is a form of bourgeoisie romanticism," one of the students explained. " In new China we strive for realism. Idealism is the opposite of realism and is therefore contrary to the principles of marxism-leninism."

I mentioned Hungary where the peoples' rebellion had just been crushed by the Russian army. The students protested vigorously against what I said. They had read in the papers that fast fascist elements had tried to seize power and deprive the Hungarian people of its freedom. This they believed.

" But let us assume that the Hungarians really were dissatisfied with the Communist government . . ."

" But how can one assume that?" interrupted the girl who was studying journalism. " The Communists are the only ones who really do something for the people. We have seen it so clearly in China—all our former governments only plundered the people. And Chairman Mao has said that the people can always distinguish between its friends and its enemies—so of course the Hungarians would never rebel against a Communist government . . ."

I changed the subject. I had heard that the students were now organized in small groups of six or seven each. Was that for political purposes?

They looked questioningly at Liang who was listening with a fatherly smile. No, one could hardly say so, replied Wu, the engineering student. There was practically no political activity at the university.

" It's to help each other," the girl studying journalism broke in. The members of a group studied together and discussed whatever problems that came up. They looked after each other —if something was wrong with one of them . . .

Something wrong—what did she mean by that.

Well, a student might have a " dark spot " in his past— maybe something he had not confessed. Or maybe deep inside he disagreed with some of the changes brought about by the Communists. Such things were bound to come out sooner or later—when he was in a bad mood, or when he lost his temper. Bad moods and fits of temper were the very symptoms one could expect from people who still held reactionary views— people who put their personal interests ahead of the group and the country . . .

" And what if you find such a dark spot in someone?"

Then they would talk to him and make him see that he was in the wrong. If he disliked something which the government had done, they would explain why it had acted as it did.

" And in the end, the student always realizes that he is in the wrong?"

" Yes, of course. After all, nobody else in the group agrees with him—the majority is against him. You can't go on thinking incorrectly."

At the end of the semester, each student has to write a report appraising himself and the members of his group. These reports are compared, and in this way it can also show if a student thinks " differently."

If he does, it will be noted down in his political dossier. This dossier tells everything that is known about the students' background and his attitude towards the new society. When he graduates from the university the dossier is sent to his employers together with his diploma. From then on it is the duty of the employer to keep the dossier up-to-date ...

But all this I learned later on from a private source. Foreigners are not given such information. Nor do they learn how the professors at China's universities were " re-educated " after the Communists came to power.

In each case, the " re-education " began with a mass meeting. The professor in question was surrounded by the students, who made accusations against him. I learned that the former president of Yenching had to answer five hundred questions prepared by his most " progressive " students. Was it not true that he had had many American friends? That he despised Marxism and believed in liberalism? That shortly before the liberation he had said to some foreign friends : " When the Communists take over I may be forced to say things which I don't mean?"

Sometimes the interrogations would continue over several weeks. The professor knew that if he did not follow the " new course "—or pretend to do so—he would lose his job and would not be able to get another one. In practically every case he ended by writing a public " confession "—he had been led astray by capitalistic and imperialistic ideas, but now he realized that Marxism was the only way for China . . .

One reads these humiliating confessions with perplexity. Some of them were written by the most brilliant men of China. Did they really mean it? One cannot ask them, but the confessions are suspiciously alike.

The universities also keep political dossiers for the professors. Once a year they have to send in reports on their political progress and to appraise the attitudes of their colleagues. If a professor is the head of a department he has a political " adviser ". Purely academic problems are left to the professor, but in all other cases he has to consult his adviser, who is a member of the Communist party or a " progressive ".

Later on I talked to a teacher whom I knew from the old

days. I promised not to use his name. That is why he dared to talk freely.

" Even when we are teaching botany or physics, we have to inject politics into it," he said. " Let's say that I tell the students that milk bottles should be sterilized. I have to add that thus one can save lives for Chairman Mao and democratic new China."

The teachers meet daily to discuss their work. They often attend each others' lectures. In this way the more progressive teachers can make sure that their colleagues have a " correct " influence on the students.

" I must admit that in some ways, education has improved," the teacher said. " We have to prepare our lectures much more thoroughly than before—if one doesn't, one will soon be found out."

The students meet regularly to discuss their teachers. If they are dissatisfied with a professor, he is asked to come and hear their complaints. Maybe he speaks indistinctly, or does not write clearly on the blackboard. Of course it is much worse if he is accused of having a " reactionary ideological attitude ".

When the Communists came to power, practically all lessons in English, French and German stopped. They were not prohibited, but everyone knew the attitude of the Communists towards the capitalist countries. Those who wanted to study their languages might easily be suspected of having reactionary views.

All over the country, people began studying Russian. Those in public positions—teachers, engineers, journalists, doctors, scientists and officials—took concentrated courses of eight hours—yes, *eight*—a day for one or two months. After a couple of years this method was dropped, however. It turned out that people forgot their Russian even faster than they had learned it.

Most of the old textbooks were replaced by Russian ones which were translated into Chinese. Once a university needed a textbook about typhoons—the violent tropical storms that rage along the China coast. The word is of Chinese origin and means " big wind ".

There were excellent works on typhoons in both Japanese and English, but they could not be used, as they had not been written by people with the " right attitude ". There are no Russian testbooks about typhoons—they do not occur in the Soviet Union—so the students had to manage without.

About a year ago the Communist leaders must have realized that education was becoming dangerously one-tracked in China. The country was isolating itself from the rest of the world by using only Soviet textbooks and by making Russian virtually the only foreign language. Chairman Mao made a speech, stating that China had much to learn from the capitalist nations. He encouraged the students to study western languages.

So now English had suddenly become popular again at the university. " But we have to start from scratch," said one of the students—in his class they had not progressed much beyond the ABC.

As a result of this new " liberalism ", Marxism had lost its all-overshadowing positions at the universities. Students of philosophy have recently resumed the study of Confucius, who had been put in a corner ever since liberation. Shortly after our arrival in Peking, workmen even began repairing the old Temple of Confucius, which had become sadly dilapidated.

But the professors have been instructed to emphasize that all the non-Marxist philosophies—the products of civilization during thousands of years—are unrealistic and false . . .

It was noon when Chi-yun and I left Yenching. As we stood near the gate, waiting for a bus, we were joined by a foreign student who was also going to town. It turned out that he was a Yugoslav. He had studied at the university for a year and spoke Chinese well.

Did he like being here? He shrugged. It was interesting, but in a way he was disappointed. Why? He looked around. There were only the three of us, so he began telling us about his experiences at the university.

Every foreign student has a Chinese " friend " who helps him with the language and gives him advice. Three months ago the students from the Eastern European countries had called a meeting with their Chinese " friends ". The Soviet

The correct way of eating rice – scoop it in with chopsticks!

Outdoor street restaurant in Peking.

students were not included—they always keep to themselves.

The foreign students were indignant. Under cover of friendship, the Chinese students had spied on them—they had written "reports" about the European students for the authorities.

The Chinese were more astonished than anything else. Why all this fuss? They wrote reports about each other all the time —why shouldn't they do so about their foreign friends?

At this point the Yugoslav was interrupted by the arrival of the bus. It was crowded as usual, so on the way back to Peking we talked about other things. One never knows who is listening—one might just as well be careful . . .

D

CHAPTER VI

Yin And Yang

MY HEAD WAS splitting and all my joints ached. Mrs. Fei was standing over me, wagging her finger.

" I told you so, but you wouldn't listen, you refused to wrap that scarf around your head! *I never catch a cold,* you said. And here you lie with a hundred and two!"

She quoted a Chinese proverb meaning *pride goes before a fall.* Before I could gather strength to answer back, Chi-yun came with the syringe. Turn around, she said—I was going to have another shot of penicillin. We always give injections to each other. Why send for the doctor? He charges money, and in nine out of ten cases he prescribes penicillin anyway . . .

" Is it wise to put all that foreign stuff into the body?"

The question came from Chang-sao, the older one of Mrs. Fei's two servants. She and I were good friends. Every evening she would bring me a bowl of hot soyabean milk. I was too skinny, she said. While it cooled off we would chat and I would tell her about life in my country. She especially liked to hear about vacuum cleaners and washing machines. Her eyes turned big and round when I described how you just put in the clothes and *buzzzz,* they are clean. Every evening she wanted to hear about the *buzzz*-machine.

" I would suggest that we call an eastern doctor for second daughter's husband," she continued. She was referring to the old-fashioned Chinese doctors. Those who have studied western medicine are called " western doctors ".

Chi-yun, who was still waiting with the syringe, took a poor view of this suggestion. In her childhood, she had had bitter experiences with Chinese medicine. It tasted abominably, she said—the very thought made her feel like throwing up. In her opinion it would be ridiculous to send for an unscientific eastern doctor when we had penicillin, the modern wonder drug.

But I was persuaded by Chang-soa's arguments. Chi-yun had already given me several injections during the last couple of days, each with some astronomical number of units. All they had done was to make the fever climb. No, then I would rather try an eastern doctor. Who knows—maybe he could help . . .

He came half an hour later, a small, unassuming man with horn-rimmed glasses. It disappointed me a little that he did not bring any of the mysterious instruments such as western doctors use. I don't know whether others feel the same way, but I love to be examined with probing and listening instruments and all the other paraphernalia of the profession.

Dr. Yen, the Chinese physician, did not even ask me to stick out my tongue and say *ah-h-h*. I was looking forward to describing my symptoms, but he only asked how my stomach was working. Then he placed my arm in a pillow and felt my pulse without even looking at a watch. His face got a faraway expression. I think more than two minutes passed.

" The other hand, please."

But why? I asked. After all, the pulse beats come from the same heart.

" Two rivers that spring from the same source may be very different."

Again he seemed to be listening to distant voices. When he was through, I produced a violent fit of coughing, but it did not seem to make any impression on him. He sat down and wrote out a prescription. I was sorry to see that he used a fountain pen. Hardly anyone writes with ink and brush any more. It looks so graceful—each character seems to spring alive—but it is too much trouble in busy new China.

Dr. Yen left instructions that the medicine was to be brewed just like tea. Drink two cups right away, two tonight, and he would be back in the morning. By then I would probably be well again, he added.

I doubted it. Deep inside I suspected him of being a

charlatan. This feeling of both wrists had made me suspicious. But anyway, it had been a cheap consultation. Dr. Yen's fee was slightly less than a shilling, and the medicine, a bagful of mysterious herbs and dry flowers, cost less than sixpence.

Next morning, when Mrs. Fei and Chi-yun looked at the thermometer, they could hardly believe their own eyes. Ninety-seven point five, and I was fit as a fiddle. Chang-sao smiled in triumph.

As soon as Dr. Yen came I began asking him questions. What was this miracle medicine he had given me? He smiled. There is nothing miraculous about Chinese medicine, he said. The doctor only tries to assist nature, the greatest of all healers.

The medicine which he had prescribed for me contained chrysanthemum flowers. That lowered the heat of the body. There was also orange peel, which was good for the digestion, certain kinds of rushes to cleanse the blood, mulberry leaves against infection, apricot seeds against cough, wheat sprouts to give strength and ginger to make me perspire.

"The human body is a part of the universe," Dr. Yen said. "It is governed by the same laws as everything else in nature. Sickness occurs when man disobeys those laws."

He was quoting from the first Chinese book on medicine which was written nearly three hundred years before Christ. *The Yellow Emperor's Inner Manual,* was the name of this great work. Its fundamental ideas have a good deal in common with Christian Science.

"The wise man does not wait until he becomes sick," the book also says. "That would be like digging a well after the thirst begins. He avoids sickness by eating the right kind of food, keeping in a good condition by exercising, and adjusting himself to changes in his surroundings."

Yin and Yang are one of the oldest Chinese symbols. It is depicted as a circle divided by an ' S '. One half is white, the other black. The white part, Yang, represents the active, male element in nature. The black part, Yin, represents the passive, female element. They are interdependent, and together they form a perfect whole which, for thousands of years, has inspired the philosophers and poets of China.

Yin and Yang also represent the basic principle in Chinese medicine, Dr. Yen said. When you become sick, it is because the balance between Yin and Yang has been upset, one of them gaining the upper hand.

The doctor's task is to restore this balance—but not by force. The human body must not be made into a battlefield. You merely try to help nature do the job. The balance between heat and cold also plays an important part in Chinese medicine. Thus a feverish patient is given a remedy that has cooling qualities, and vice versa . . .

" But this is only a rough outline," Dr. Yen said with a smile. " When I was fifteen, I became apprentice to a famous doctor. My education was not completed until I was twenty-five."

During those ten years, Dr. Yen had made a thorough study of the Chinese flora. Chinese medicine consists mainly of herbs, barks, roots and flowers. He spent a year in humid, cloudy Szechuan province which lies close to the border of Tibet. Szechuan means *Four Rivers*—it is here, they say, that the dogs bark when they see the sun. Most of China's medicinal herbs and fungi come from this province.

Every " eastern " doctor knows thousands of traditional prescriptions by heart. Many of these prescriptions have been used for over two thousand years, but new remedies and combinations are constantly being found, for Chinese medicine is today in a state of rapid development.

The Yellow Emperor's Inner Manual has a detailed description of how to take the pulse and make a diagnosis. The book says that two patients who have exactly the same symptoms may need entirely different treatments. Each case must be diagnosed and treated separately. " Eastern " doctors do not prescribe patent medicines.

They hardly ever use surgery, but it does happen. Ancient Chinese history tells of a warrior who was hit by an arrow. The arrowhead lodged in a bone and caused inflammation. The doctor who treated the case first rubbed the wound with plant juices which numbed it—a kind of local anaesthetic. The warrior played chess while the bone was laid bare and scraped clean. Then the doctor sewed up the wound.

As early as 700 B.C. Chinese doctors used massage for certain kinds of rheumatism. During epidemics of rabies they recommended the killing of all dogs. Some metabolistic disorders were cured with seaweed which regulated the function of the thyroid gland. Patients suffering from diabetes were put on a strict diet very similar to the one now used by western doctors. Tetanus was diagnosed in ancient China, but it was not known how to prevent or cure it.

Shortly before Christ, Chinese doctors began to treat skin diseases with sulphur and mercury. Not until the sixteenth century did European doctors learn to use this treatment. The Chinese were also the first to use chaulmoogra oil against leprosy.

For religious reasons it was forbidden to perform autopsies in ancient China—the ancestral spirits would have been upset if the bodies of the dead had come to them in a mutilated state. Yet more than two thousand years ago the Chinese doctors calculated correctly the length of the intestinal canal.

During an epidemic in the year 510, the first hospital was established in China. Half a century later there were government hospitals in all the large cities. From the seventh to the ninth century China was the centre of medical learning in the East. There was a medical school with three hundred and fifty students in the capital, and the lectures were attended by Korean, Japanese and Arabian doctors who had come here to be trained as specialists.

In the sixteenth century, smallpox appeared in China after having taken a fearful toll of human lives in Europe. For a while the disease raged unchecked, but then the Chinese doctors learned how to prevent it. They took a little pus from the boils of an affected person, dried it and blew it into the nostrils of those who were well. Several hundred years passed before the West learned to vaccinate.

Chinese medicine had begun to decline long before the smallpox epidemic. This was largely due to the strong influence of Taoism, upon the medical profession. Taoism originally a profound philosophy, had in time degenerated into a religion dominated by mysticism and witchcraft. The Taoists were obsessed by the desire to make an elixir which would give man immortality. Like the alchemists of Europe, they believed it possible to make gold.

It was only natural that the Chinese doctors were drawn into these experiments. They were the only ones who had any knowledge of chemistry. Exorcism had always played a certain role, even though a modest one, within Chinese medicine. Now it became one of the most important factors. As a result, the philosophers of China, who have always been great realists, came to despise the medical profession. That is probably why chemistry and physics have never been developed in China. The Chinese invented gunpowder, but used it only for fireworks.

When my wife was a child, the old-fashioned Chinese doctors were despised by all modern Chinese. In 1929, shortly after Chiang Kai-shek had come to power, a law was even passed prohibiting them from practising. But before it became effective, the three hundred thousand old-fashioned doctors of China rose in protest. It was they who tended eighty per cent of the sick, they argued—if they were not allowed to practise, it would be a catastrophe for the country.

Only when the old-fashioned doctors threatened to march on the capital did Chiang Kai-shek give in. This did not mean that they had found favour in his eyes, however. He had just been converted to Christianity, and the foreign missionaries told him that Chinese medicine was allied with the devil. If the missionary doctors had bothered to find out what it was they attacked, they might have discovered that they themselves could have learned quite a lot from the old-fashioned Chinese doctors.

" When Chiang Kai-shek was in power I could hardly make a living," Dr. Yen told me. For a while it looked as if the profession would die out. Who wanted to study for more than ten years in order to become a member of a despised and ill-paid profession?

When the Communists took over, the picture changed. " We old-fashioned doctors are deeply grateful to Chairman Mao,"

Dr. Yen said. I could tell that he really meant it and he had reason to.

Since 1949, the profession has again become highly respected. Last year an institute for the study of Chinese medicine was established. So far there are only eighty students, but the number will be doubled every year, and similar schools are being established in all the larger cities. The study of western medicine is being continued, but for one year the students have to attend one of the new institutes in order to study their own country's ancient art of healing. Similarly, the old-fashioned doctors now receive part of their training in schools of western medicine.

The Communist plan is to make the twain meet, so that there will no longer be eastern and western doctors, but just *doctors* who have learned the best from both schools.

No doctors in China have private practice any more. All are employed by the state. Thus, Dr. Yen worked at an old-fashioned Chinese pharmacy which had been taken over by the government. He got the same salary as western-style doctors.

He told us that the students of western medicine who attend the new institute have been amazed by many of the things they have learned. At first they would hardly believe it when told that outside of Peking, there are six different kinds of plants growing which are more effective against malaria than quinine. All the hospitals in China have recently adopted an ancient cure against tapeworm.

" I must admit that here you turn the human body into a battlefield," Dr. Yen said with a smile. " The patient is given pumpkin seeds mixed with a certain kind of betel nut. Half an hour later the worm comes out."

There is another kind of " cure " which the Chinese have used since time immemorial. When they have a fever, they pinch and pull the skin of the throat or the back so violently that it leaves blue stripes ...

This reminds me of something that happened when Chi-yun and I were on our way to Red China. There was a Chinese crew on the ship, and when we came to Bombay a sick sailor was sent to the hospital. The chief mate and the Indian doctor who was called agreed that it was a serious case of *sub-cutaneous haemorrhage*. In ordinary language that means bleeding under the skin.

Chi-yun and I visited the sailor at the hospital. We expected to find him dying, but he was sitting up in bed, protesting loudly because the ship was about to leave without him. "There is nothing wrong with me," he said—"just a touch of fever."

The doctor came. He insisted that the man was dangerously ill. As a proof he pointed to the sailor's throat. Just look at those blue marks . . .

The sailor could not speak English. With my wife acting as interpreter, he finally succeeded in making the doctor understand that he had made the blue lines himself. At first, the doctor refused to believe it—like everyone else, he hated to admit a mistake—but when we returned to the ship the sailor was walking with us, whistling happily . . .

"We don't recommend this kind of home-treatment," Dr. Yen said. "But there can be cases where it helps. The effect is somewhat like blood-letting."

Strangest of all the treatments handed down from ancient times is *acupuncture*—puncturing of the body with needles. Chi-yun and I visited a clinic in Peking where eighty-five doctors specialize in this treatment, the effects of which has astounded western doctors.

"Maybe *that* can be called a miracle-cure," Dr. Yen said. "Although we have used this method for a couple of thousand years, we still don't know why it is so effective. My own theory is that the pricking somehow stimulates the nerve centres."

At the clinic we saw a patient groaning from a toothache. The doctor pushed two very fine needles into his jaw. It did not seem to hurt at all. A few seconds later the patient relaxed visibly. The pain was gone.

When Dr. Yen began practising—that was in the early 'twenties—Chinese women were very old-fashioned. They would not undress for the doctor, so he gave them the needle-treatment through the clothes. Even so the doctor was by no means working blindly. Students of acupuncture must practise for years on metal dummies which have holes in all the places where it can be beneficial to stimulate the nerves—three hundred and sixty-five altogether. The first such dummies were made more than a thousand years ago.

Of course acupuncture is not effective against everything, but there seems to be hardly any disease on which it does not have a beneficial influence. A doctor of western medicine whom we knew had suffered from insomnia for years. The sleeping pills which he took had made him a nervous wreck. He was persuaded to try acupuncture.

Since then he has had no trouble falling asleep, though he no longer takes pills. Another patient was cured of sleepwalking after three treatments.

People suffering from stomach ulcers also show improvement, and victims of infantile paralysis have regained use of some of their muscles. An incredibly fat Hungarian who was visiting Peking lost forty pounds after two months of treatment. Even patients with malignant malaria often improve.

In some cases the needles are pushed through the whole body, but usually only the skin is pierced. The needles, made of gold, silver or stainless steel, are left in for from five to twenty minutes.

During the last few years, several Soviet doctors have received acupuncture treatment in Peking. In France, a few doctors have begun to use the treatment. It has been popular for many years in Japan.

Couldn't I try it? Dr. Yen smiled and shook his head. It was only for sick people, and there was nothing wrong with me. " Remember—eat plenty of vegetables, not too much meat. Exercise every day, and do not let small things get on your nerves. Then you will not need a doctor any more."

He got up and bowed. As soon as he had left the room I jumped out of bed. It was wonderful to be well again.

CHAPTER VII

A Tree In The Forest

ONE DAY WHEN I was out walking in Peking I saw a face which seemed familar to me. Yes, it was Chen-ming—one of my best friends from my schooldays at Yenching. Many a night we had sat and talked until I became hoarse. He was not the most brilliant of my schoolmates, but he was a warm-hearted fellow, surprisingly straightforward for a Chinese.

I hurried after him, but when I caught up with him I hesi-tated for a moment. Twice since our arrival I had met old friends who hurried away as soon as we had said hello. What if Chen-ming did the same?

But his face lit up the moment he saw me. We slapped each other on the back, and for several minutes we stood talking eagerly in the icy wind. Then we discovered that we were both shivering with cold.

"Let's go somewhere." Chen-ming looked at his watch. His long, sensitive face was thinner than before. "I'm usually attending some meeting at this time, but today I happen to be free. I know a good restaurant near the market."

In the old days he would have invited me to his home. The Chinese seldom do that nowadays. Most people share a house with several other families, and few have servants, so it is not convenient to entertain. Besides, your neighbours keep an eye on you. The fewer strangers you bring home with you, the less attention you attract.

You usually have to wait a while at the restaurants of crowded Peking, but we were lucky and got a table right away. When Chen-ming took off his fur cap I saw that his hair was beginning to turn grey. Usually, the Chinese don't get grey hair until their late fifties. One hardly ever sees baldheaded Chinese.

We talked about our schooldays together. Before long the conversation turned to Wei, who had been Chen-ming's roommate at the university. Chen-ming had not seen him for several years, but he had heard that he was doing very well. He held a high government position in Shanghai. He was a member of the Communist party.

" Are you a Communist, too?"

" No."

" Then maybe you can help me . . ." I explained my problem. In my youth I had spent six years in China. I knew the language fairly well, yet today I felt like a complete stranger. So did my wife, though she was born here. Everybody had changed while we were away—people were more serious and intent than before. It was impossible for us to get close to them any more.

" I want to know if people really believe in this new system," I said. Chen-ming looked thoughtfully at me.

" It's no use to ask a Communist such a question," I continued. " They all give the same answer. And those who don't preach Marxism, say nothing at all."

" Yes," Chen-ming said, " it isn't easy to know where people stand today. Quite a few have undoubtedly been convinced by Communism, but there are also many opportunists. You have a much better chance of getting ahead if you are a party member. And there are also some who echo the Communists just to be left in peace."

" Yes, that's typically Chinese," I remarked. " Avoid conflict at any price."

Chen-ming frowned. " I remember that you also said things like that when we studied together. You thought that we Chinese were moral cowards—yes, you did, Karl! And in a way you're right—we're scared of losing face, and when we get excited about something we try not to show it. But you're mistaken if you think that the Communists won because nobody dared to resist them!"

He leaned eagerly over the table. Now he looked more like

the old Chen-ming. " What about the war against Japan? Fifty million Chinese left their homes on the coast and walked into the interior because they did not want to compromise with the Japanese. Was that cowardly? And just after the war, when Chiang tried to silence those who disagreed with him, we defied him, didn't we? I suppose you've heard that several students from our university were shot by Chiang's secret police. They were after me, too. I had to flee to Hong Kong."

He was a chemical engineer and succeeded in getting a good job in Hong Kong. His voice turned wistful when he told me about what a wonderful time he had had in the British colony —a big apartment, servants, a car.

" I used to tell myself that the civil war on the mainland was none of my business," he continued. " I really felt like staying on in Hong Kong, but I just couldn't. Somehow, I was ashamed of myself. It was as if I had failed my country."

In 1952, three years after the Communists came to power, Chen-ming went home. He was received with open arms in Red China. The government paid for his trip back, and in Peking he was invited to live at a hostel for returned students. He did not have to search for a job. Representatives of various government organizations came to him with offers.

" Of course they couldn't offer me nearly as much as I had made in Hong Kong. After all, China is a poor country. Now I get only one hundred and twenty yuan (about eighteen pounds sterling) a month, but I don't mind that at all. You see, my work really interests me here . . ."

I have heard many say the same thing in new China— even people who are not the least bit interested in politics. They were so tired of the endless civil wars and the corruption. Now they finally have a strong, united China to work for.

There was even a chance that Chen-ming's present salary would be reduced. At his office, they had just started holding meetings to discuss a general adjustment of salaries. Everybody was asked to state whether he thought he was getting a fair wage compared to the others. In the end, an entirely new wage scale would be decided upon by vote.

There was also a new spirit of helpfulness which appealed to

Chen-ming. " I am consulted by those who are less experienced than I. In turn, I get help from those who have a higher education. Many people learn to read and write according to the same principle—*to sweep away blindness,* we call this literacy campaign."

New China has also tried to put a stop to bureaucracy and office tyranny. " You know what I mean—the type that licks the boss' boots and bullies his subordinates. Just like Mr. Cheng . . ."

We both smiled. Mr. Cheng had been the most disliked of our teachers.

" People like him don't have much chance in China any more," Chen-ming continued. Every office now has a special box for letters of criticism. If there is anything you find unjust you only have to complain. Something is sure to be done about it if the complaint is justified.

This, by the way, is an ancient custom in China. Anyone who wanted to make a complaint to the Emperor, could strike a bell hanging outside the palace. Chinese history tells how one of the early Emperors was interrupted three times during breakfast by the complaint-bell.

On the other hand, Chen-ming thought that there were too many political meetings. After working for a whole day, one did not always feel like listening to a long lecture on Marxism.

But on the whole he got along well in new China. About a year after his return, however, something happened that brought about a great change in his life. At one of the regular political meetings, the conversation turned to those who still held reservations about the new government. One of Chen-ming's superiors, a Communist, stood up and pointed at him.

" You still have doubts," he said. " I have often felt that you are not really one of us. Deep inside, you are not convinced that Marxism is the best thing for China."

At this point one of Chen-ming's colleagues, a Communist, stood up to speak. " I had always got along well with him," Chen-ming told me. " I rather thought that he liked me, but you should have heard what he said about me! I always went my own way, I lacked the collective attitude, at heart I was still a bourgeois.

"When he was through, others took over. Everyone had something to say against me—I was too individualistic, I was a typical product of the upper classes. You can't imagine how awful it was to sit there and listen to them. I had never felt so alone."

Finally Chen-ming jumped up and protested. "You talk as if I were a traitor to my country," he said. "But it isn't true! I'm a patriot—otherwise I wouldn't have come back from Hong Kong. I can't help it if I come from a wealthy family . . ."

Here he was interrupted. He was mistaken—all members of the former upper classes must share the blame because the poor had been exploited and China sold to the imperialist powers. It was a collective guilt.

"But what do you want me to do?" Chen-ming asked. They replied that he must put a stop to his individualistic divergencies. He must be firm as a rock in his belief in Marxism. He must learn to think like a worker, to consider all problems from a worker's point of view.

Again Chen-ming protested. He had never been a worker, nor had the others who were present. Why then pretend that they could think like workers? It was a plain fact that no members of the working classes had received a proper education. Why should people try to think like uneducated persons?

There was a shocked silence. Then Chen-ming's boss rose and said that Chen-ming's last words had confirmed their suspicions. He did indeed harbour anti-democratic tendencies. He did not understand that only the members of the working class were capable of making pure and unselfish sacrifices for the revolution. He had no confidence in the workers. This meant that he had no confidence in new China, in the Communist party, in Chairman Mao.

"You despise the lower classes," his boss said. "But remember that the lower classes are the people, and the people are China."

It was almost midnight before the meeting was over. When

Chen-ming went to bed that night he could not sleep. He kept seeing himself surrounded by people who pointed accusingly at him.

Was he really as bad as they had tried to make him? He had to admit to himself that he was selfish. One could not say that of the Communists. They demanded great sacrifices from others, but they certainly did not spare themselves either. They had done so much for China. If they were dissatisfied with him it must be because there was something wrong with him . . .

The next meeting took place on the following evening. First someone made an enthusiastic speech about the tremendous development that had taken place under the Communists. All China was marching steadfastly towards socialism—but there were many obstacles ahead, there were both external and internal enemies . . .

Again Chen-ming found himself under fire. He did not take Marxism seriously enough, they said. He considered it only one of many political theories—he refused to face the fact that the final victory of Marxism was predetermined by history . . .

" I tried to defend myself," Chen-ming said, " but it wasn't easy. When people have studied dialectical materialism they can turn anything you say against you. And a lot of what they said was very convincing. I came to realize that there really *was* something wrong with my attitude. As the Communists put it, the opinion of ten is worth more than the opinion of one, and the opinion of a hundred people is worth more than the opinion of ten. How could I put my own opinion above everybody else's ?"

They taught him that even when the Communists do something that seems wrong, one must remember that they are the only ones who have the good of the people at heart. " Don't single out one tree," they told him. " Look at the whole forest."

They asked him not to make things so difficult for himself. " You are nervous and worried. That is because you try to solve your problems alone. Join us—then it will be so much easier. Take the hand that the people extend to you."

What they grow on their "private" piece of ground the farmers are allowed to sell in the towns.

The spring festival is celebrated also in Communist China.

Every evening they would gather to help Chen-ming day after day, week after week. They explained to him that he must never give way to his whims. " Your impulses are rooted in the past, so they are dangerous. When you get a sudden impulse, stop it and analyze it. Every thought must be carefully weighed. Always ask yourself : am I looking at this from my own selfish point of view or from the point of view of the masses ?"

Chen-ming suddenly sounded tired. He was staring at a crack in the table. " It isn't easy to think like that. You have to be on guard all the time. You must suppress your own thoughts—it is like killing something inside yourself. But it seems to be the only way out. And it is true what they told me—that once you learn to do it, everything becomes easier. Then you can get peace of mind."

" So you have learned to think that way ?"

" Yes." He was still staring at the crack. " Almost. Doubts do come up every once in a while, I must admit—but that's the way it ought to be. The class-struggle must be fought inside every one of us. You must keep fighting your own selfishness, the way you weed your garden. But most of the time I am quite happy. My work has never meant so much to me before."

" You said that sometimes you feel doubtful. What do you mean by that ?"

" It is hard to explain." He shook his head. " But sometimes it seems to me that there is something machine-like about this way of life—it is all logic and principles and production. And there is no real friendship any more—not like in the old days. You never talk to anyone about the things that really matter. It's true that they ask us to speak freely at the meetings, but there are many things one doesn't like to speak about in front of so many.

" And then you never know when you can trust any more. Not that I am afraid of spies or anything like that, and you won't get shot because your criticize, but . . ." He hesitated. " Now take the first meeting when they said that I was too individualistic. For a whole year they had been taking note of

E

everything I said. They had written reports about me. Of course I realize that they only did it to help me, and afterwards they were very nice to me again. But an experience like that makes you think twice before you open your mouth. Sometimes I feel like cracking a joke or saying something crazy, just for the hell of it—but I don't. Maybe someone is going to remember it. And anyway, it would of course be foolish and unconstructive."

Did he never speculate about politics any more? Not very often, but it happened. He had worried a great deal about Hungary, for instance. First the papers sided with Nagy. The former government had misunderstood Marxism, the editorials said. That was why a cleft had developed between the government and the people, but now the mistake was being corrected. This only proved that true Marxists were not afraid of admitting their mistakes and learning by them.

But when the Red Army returned to Budapest, the editors suddenly changed their minds. Now the brave revolutionaries had become hooligans and fascists. Chen-ming hardly knew what to believe any more . . .

"I'm afraid I have to go now," he said, rising. "It was wonderful to see you again—almost like the old days. One never gets into a good discussion any more—everybody has the same opinion. But of course that's only good," he quickly added. "We must have unity in China—otherwise we cannot build a new, just society and at the same time catch up with the rest of the world."

We did not make a date to meet again, but on a Sunday afternoon a couple of weeks later we bumped into each other at the Peking Zoo. He was with a group of people, so we didn't get a chance to talk much.

"Do you still feel doubtful about Hungary?" I asked. He smiled and asked if I hadn't read the circular which was issued by the Central Committee just after Christmas.

I had. "More on the historical experience of the dictatorship of the proletariat," it was called. It urged people to be on guard against the propaganda of the enemy. "The fundamental problem is and remains the struggle between the imperialist-reactionary block and the democratic camp of the socialists. . . All those who have accepted the viewpoint of the people must distinguish clearly between the differences within the socialist family and the differences between ourselves and the external enemy . . . However many twists and turns await us on our forward journey, humanity will eventually reach its bright destiny—Communism."

" This circular has been thoroughly explained to us at the latest meetings," Chen-ming continued. " Now I know what to believe. There have been errors committed in Hungary, but we must not centre our attention on that. The unity of the socialist countries comes first. You mustn't look only at one tree—you must see the whole forest."

We shook hands. I watched him as he walked off and was lost in the crowd.

CHAPTER VIII

The Darlings Of Mao Tse-Tung

IF THERE IS anything more boring than writing about a factory, it is to visit one. Chi-yun and I were therefore prepared for the worst that day we went out to the National Spinning Mill No. 2—but there was a pleasant surprise in store for us.

First there was the inevitable tour. We wandered past miles of clacking machines, accompanied by a female secretary who filled us with statistics. There were five thousand workers at the factory. They produced two hundred and forty thousand yards of cotton cloth a day. Each year the government was building four new cotton spinneries with the same capacity as this one. China, once an importer of cotton cloth, now exported it to several of the South Asian countries . . .

I tried to listen intelligently, but suddenly the secretary broke off in the middle of a description of a complicated chemical process.

" I am afraid this doesn't interest you very much. Is there anything special you would like to hear about?"

" Yes," I replied with a smile, " something less technical, something, uh—something romantic. But I suppose one doesn't find that at a cotton mill?"

" Something romantic?" She brightened. " Oh, yes—you could talk to Comrade Liang. I think the story of her marriage is very romantic."

We found her in the day nursery where she was suckling her baby daughter. Seen through European eyes it was not a very impressive place. The cement floor was bare, the stove smoked. But one should bear in mind that public welfare was practically non-existent in China before the liberation. It was

68

not unusual for factory girls to work with their babies bound to their backs. Now there are nurseries and kindergartens at every large institution in the country.

Comrade Liang was not at all embarrassed by our sudden arrival. She just went on suckling her child. The Chinese are very natural about such things. She was small and plump, and two dimples appeared on her cheeks when she told us about how she had met her husband.

It was at a union convention. She had already read about him in the papers, for he was a famous workers' hero who regularly overfulfilled his quota. She was only a model worker, which is one degree lower, but nothing to sniff at for a girl of nineteen.

The papers said afterwards that their immediate interest for each other was due to " mutual admiration for their unselfish sacrifices in the service of the Chinese people ". I wonder whether the dimples didn't have something to do with it, too. In any case it was love at first sight.

Did they get married right away? No—after the convention meeting she did not hear a word from him for more than a month. She smiled at the thought of how nervous and worried she had been. Her work even suffered—one day there was a fault in a roll of cloth from one of her machines.

" Her comrades offered to take the blame," the secretary put in. " They were proud of her record and wanted to keep it unblemished, but Comrade Liang firmly rejected this proposal . . ."

" Why didn't you hear from him?" I asked. She explained that he was a member of the Communist party. As soon as the convention was over he told his " cell " what had happened. They wrote to the chief of personnel at her factory. True, she was a model worker, but even so they wanted to know about her background. Fortunately it turned out that her attitude had always been correct, so the cell gave him its blessings, and then he came and proposed . . .

When Comrade Liang was through feeding the baby she offered to show us her home. We accompanied her to a large group of buildings opposite the factory. They reminded me of the workers' dwellings that were built in northern Europe around the turn of the century. Though the houses were only a year and a half old they already had a slight atmosphere of slum. Here and there the plaster was falling down from the walls, the paint peeling off. When one considers how much the Chinese have built during the last few years, it is not surprising that the quality has suffered.

On the way she showed us the school, the clinic and the big dining-hall where you could get a good meal for less than a shilling. Some of the workers came over and chatted with the secretary and Comrade Liang. They were free and easy in their manners; there was none of the former servility of their class. Everybody was dressed alike. It was a classless society, void of tradition. It was China's new proletariat.

Mao-Tse-tung seldom makes a speech without putting in a few words of praise for the workers. " The advance guard of the revolution ", he calls them. I suppose he does so to give them self-confidence. If one takes a close look at the Chinese revolution, one soon discovers that it was not led by the workers —they did not even form the rear-guard.

The Chinese Communist Party was formed in the beginning of the 'twenties. It was sponsored by the Soviet Union and all important decisions were made in Moscow. Now, the writings of Marx and Lenin clearly say that only the city proletariat can make revolutions, so the Chinese Communists concentrated on organizing the workers in large towns.

It soon turned out that China's tiny working class lacked " political consciousness ". Their wages were pitifully small, but they were fairly well off compared to the farmers. The majority of them turned a deaf ear to the Communist call for a class struggle. The people were tired of civil war. They wanted peace.

Chiang Kai-shek appealed to the awakening nationalism of China. That was why he won the first round in the struggle with the Communists. Towards the end of the 'twenties, when the Reds started rebellions in several cities, Chiang suppressed them ruthlessly. For a while it looked as if the Communist movement would die out in China.

It was then that one of the Chinese Communist leaders began to think independently. Mao Tse-tung asked himself if the Russian methods were suited for China. Would it not be better to organize the peasants? There were so many of them; they were dissatisfied and had something to fight for . . .

Such thoughts were heresy for a Marxist, and when Mao carried them out he was condemned by Moscow. Despite this he persisted. During the next fifteen years, the Red flag waved only in the countryside.

Pursued by Chiang's forces, the Communists made their famous " Long March ". Though Chiang received help from the West, he could not " wipe out the Red bandits ", as he kept promising to do. During this period the Communists received no help from Russia, yet they grew stronger. They thrived on the discontent of the farmers. Mao Tse-tung had been right after all.

During the long war with Japan the Communists became ardent nationalists and fought against the common enemy. But when Japan was beaten, civil war flared up again. Chiang held the cities, Mao was master in the country. Now one should think that he would give the farmers credit for his final victory. But when his armies had captured the cities, he told the surprised workers that it was *they* who had won the revolution! Many of them scarcely knew that a revolution had taken place. The farmers now took second place. They were not " politically reliable," Mao said—they lack the solidarity and sacrificing spirit of the working class, for every farmer, however poor, is a potential capitalist.

Soon after the land distribution, the farmers began buying and selling land. The Communists realized that a new class of landowners would appear. This was probably why a little over a year ago Mao Tse-tung decided to collectivize the farms —despite the fact that Khrushchev had just admitted that the Soviet collectives had not been a success. Khrushchev's speech was not published in China.

Today, all the heaviest burdens rest on the farmers. They get less to eat than the city people. They have to work as hard as ever—in some cases even harder. The land which Mao

promised them and gave them as a reward for their help in the
revolution, has been taken away from them again. They know
that the workers have a much higher standard of living than
they, so many of them try to go to the cities to get jobs at the
new factories—but they are refused. They have to stay on the
land and raise the products needed to pay for industrializing
the country . . .

When you tell the Chinese Communist that many of their
countrymen are afraid of expressing themselves freely, they
reply that at least this is not true of the workers. No, of course
not, for generally speaking they have nothing to complain
about. The are the apple of Mao Tse-tung's eye.

Thus, Comrade Liang made twelve pounds a month, or
about three times as much as a farmer. She paid only six
shillings a month for her one-room apartment. True, there was
only one small window, and the cement floor and bare walls
reminded me of a cellar—but there was central heating, there
was running water and even a flush toilet. Her husband, the
workers' hero, made fourteen pounds a month.

She saw him only once a week, when he came to spend the
night. He worked at another factory, and their weekly day off
did not fall on the same day. " But maybe we'll get a summer
vacation next year," she said hopefully. The Chinese workers
only get a day off on October 1st, the anniversary of the
People's Republic, on May 1st, and at Chinese new year.

Many of the married workers had their parents living with
them. But the family relationship had changed quite a bit since
the days when the young people brought their wages home to
their parents. The old people now looked after the children,
if they did not have a job themselves. They got food, lodging
and a little pocket money. The young ones were their own
bosses.

Around seventy per cent of the workers at the mill were
girls. The unmarried ones lived in dormitories, six to each
room. Most of the space was taken up by the beds, but the
walls were plastered with pictures of film stars.

Only about seventy-five per cent of those employed at the
factory did productive work. The rest were bookkeepers, clerks

or political propaganda workers. At some Chinese industrial institutions the percentage of administrative personnel is even higher. Many of the offices I have been to were crowded with people who seemed to have difficulties in making the time pass. About a year ago, the Communist leaders vowed that they were going to reduce this army of personnel, but they have not done so yet. It is not easy in a country where everything is as centralized as in China.

All the workers belonged to the same union. Did this union have much power? Certainly, replied both Comrade Liang and the secretary, but when I questioned them further it turned out that the workers' rights did not go much beyond Article 4 of the Trade Union Law. The first and foremost duty of the unions is to educate and organize the masses of workers and staff members to support the laws and desires of the Peoples' Government and to carry out the policies of the Peoples' Government in order to consolidate the peoples' state power . . .

In the transition period before the state nationalized Chinese industry and business, the workers were encouraged to strike. " Now it is quite unthinkable that the workers should want to do so," the secretary said. " After all, we have a peoples' government in China—the workers would not want to strike against themselves."

Comrade Liang was a member of the managing committee of the union, and she told us about its social activities. There were recreation centres for sick workers. Once a week, the union organized a social evening with dancing. Uneducated workers could pass high school examinations by attending night school. There were daily meetings at which the policies of the government were explained. The union also helped workers who had large families and found it hard to make ends meet.

" Some weeks ago, the union started a birth control campaign," Comrade Liang went on. Chi-yun and I looked at her in surprise, and the secretary gave a start and protested. The leaders of new China are extremely sensitive where birth control is concerned. Not long ago they condemned it as " capitalist nonsense " and " a vicious way of killing the people without spilling blood ".

For years the Chinese Communists have maintained that birth control is unnecessary. China is not over-populated, they say—it is a matter of under-production. All the densely-populated countries of Asia have such a low standard of living because the upper-classes exploit the poor, runs the Communist argument. The distribution of wealth is unjust—and that cannot be denied.

But Comrade Liang admitted that a problem remained although the distribution of wealth was now more just in China. Before the liberation, the mortality rate was one hundred and seventeen per one thousand in some Chinese cities. It has since gone down to forty-four per thousand. A survey among seven thousand female workers at a factory showed that one thousand nine hundred of them became pregnant in one year. Each woman gets fifty-six days off with full pay for her confinement, so this means a great loss of manpower.

The standard of living of the workers has not improved very much although their average monthly income has risen from eight pounds five shillings before the liberation to ten pounds sixteen shillings today. The main reason for this is the large number of children. Each year, there are fifteen million more Chinese than the year before. Despite all the progress under the Communists, the advances in production can hardly keep pace with the growth in population . . .

I asked the secretary why she had objected when Comrade Liang used the word *birth-control*. She claimed that it was an incorrect way of expressing it.

"The cultural standard of the workers has been raised under the democratic leadership of the Communists," she said. "Therefore, the workers have realized the advantage of not having too large a family. The people have asked their leaders for help, and the desire of the people now being the will of the government, a campaign to teach mothers proper spacing of children has been started . . ."

Comrade Liang told us about an ancient Chinese way of avoiding conception. One only has to swallow a couple of dozen live tadpoles. She had heard that it was quite effective, but as far as she knew it was hardly ever used any more.

She added that not only the unions taught birth-con . . .
She checked herself in time. " Teach the mothers proper
spacing," she said instead of the forbidden word. The farmers'
associations have started a similar movement in the country.
They show film which point out the advantages of planned
parenthood. Several million leaflets with graphic illustrations
have been distributed.

" Has it had any effect ?"

It was too soon to tell. Comrade Liang said that the union
now offered a course in planned parenthood. About one
quarter of the married workers had signed up for this course.

" That's not very much," I commented.

" No, the desire to have many children is very strong in
China." Life had been so uncertain in the old days. If a man
had many children, there was more chance that one of them
would get ahead and could support his parents in their old age.
It was difficult to change this attitude . . .

Before we left, I asked Comrade Liang is she had signed
up for the new course in planned parenthood. No, she replied,
not yet . . .

" My husband wants to have at least two sons before we
begin to think about that."

CHAPTER IX

Old Horse

HIS REAL NAME was Ma Wen-teh, but probably no one in the village knew it. Everybody called him Lao Ma—Old Horse. It suited him very well, for his long, bony face somehow made one think of the tough, northern Chinese ponies.

It was said that the gods had spared Lao Ma for so long because he knew how to make them laugh. He had known hard times in his life, but the bitterness did not go inside of him and eat him up—it glanced off his impervious humour. Though over seventy, he was hale and hearty and could take his turn with the young men in the field.

Nobody could spin a yarn like Lao Ma. Even the wandering story-tellers who occasionally came to the village were no match for him, although they added drama to their tales by beating a drum. When he paused to stuff his long-stemmed bamboo pipe, the listeners would wring their hands with impatience. He could imitate all imaginable sounds, from the weird cries of the spirits to the mutter of the river which would sometimes rise to thunder.

The river was the villain in many of his stories. On the night he was born, the water of the river had lapped against his mother's bedstead. Everybody else had fled—only her husband stayed with her and watched the water creep higher and higher up the bricklaid platform—the *kang*—which is the bed of the farmers. But when Lao Ma's first wail rent the air, the water began to recede—or so it was said.

Lao Ma liked best to tell about the times of long ago. Perhaps it was because he could then give his imagination a freer rein, for on one else in the village could remember much from the days of the Manchu emperors. Or perhaps it was because youth and childhood always seem to come closer as time moves us further away from them.

In the days of the Dragon Throne, representatives of the Emperor had come to tame the river—learned men who had studied books about the evil deeds of the river in past generations. They mobilized armies of farmers from the area around the river. With their small baskets the farmers carried mountains of earth and stones to dikes which were to prevent the river from running wild.

In those days, five or six, even seven years would sometimes pass without the river overflowing. But in the meanwhile it was gathering strength. Slowly, inch by inch, it raised itself on its own deposits of mud. When it finally broke through it took a terrible revenge for all the time it had been imprisoned. Three times during Lao Ma's childhood the people had had to seek refuge on the hills half a day's journey south.

But there was always one compensation, Lao Ma concluded when he told about the flights from the river. The bigger the flood, the thicker the layer of fertile mud left behind on the fields. The next harvest was always bountiful, as if it had drawn nourishment from the misfortunes of the people.

Also in those days officials would come once a year and take away a part of the harvest. On the other hand, when famine threatened after a flood the government would open its granaries. During the last years of the Manchu dynasty, however, the granaries would often be empty. The officials became corrupt, work on the dikes had to be discontinued for lack of funds, and from the south came rumours of attempts to overthrow the Manchus.

At that time there were two wealthy families in the village —Wang and Yao. They were big landowners, and the roofs on their farms were made of tiles instead of the usual straw. During hard times, or when there was a wedding or a funeral, the villagers would come to them to borrow money. A man could get into debt for life because he had to bury his father or mother or marry off a daughter.

At the Wang's you could also rent the fine red sedan chair in which the bride was carried to the groom's home. When she stepped out of the chair her face was covered by a silk scarf—red, for that was the colour of happiness. Her husband was not to see her face until the moment they drank from the same cup in front of the ancestral altar. Then they were man and wife.

Lao Ma's family was not so poor in those days. They owned a piece of land that measured two hundred long strides in either direction. The earth in this district was so rich that you could harvest grain twice a year and vegetables three times. Lao Ma's leg muscles were hard as stone from pedalling the treadmill with which you lifted the river water into the fields during the dry season. In the late autumn the farmers would bury the vegetables—first they were covered with a layer of leaves, then with half a fathom of earth. In this way they kept fresh and free from frost all winter.

Lao Ma had two brothers, and when his father died the land was divided. Each brother married and had children, and soon there were so many mouths that the fields could hardly feed them even during good years. When there was a flood and the harvest was ruined, it was impossible to exist until the next harvest. Thus it came about that not only Lao Ma, but also his brothers had to borrow money from Wang and Yao. If one was not careful the debt would multiply by itself. It was difficult to scrape up enough money to pay the yearly interest, and virtually impossible to reduce the debt.

In the last days of the dynasty, the officials demanded so much of the grain that a family could hardly manage on what was left. The villagers got a little cash from selling vegetables in the nearest town, but the money went as quickly as it came. There were so many things that had to be bought—salt, cloth for shoes and garments, oil for the lamp, and a little tobacco if times were not too hard.

Many families kept a pig which lived on refuse from the kitchen and what it could find in the fields. There was great excitement when the pig was taken to the market to be sold. When Lao Ma was big enough he helped to carry the squealing animal which was tied by its legs to a pole—it wouldn't do to let it run off some of its weight on the way.

The farmers themselves could not afford to eat meat—they only had a taste of it at weddings or funerals or during the New year festival which in those days lasted for two weeks. During the rest of the year they ate little but the dry, yellow cornbread which they washed down with cabbage soup. They also made *dofu* : soyabean that is ground and made into a white cheese. It is nourishing, but has little taste except when fried, and the farmers could seldom afford cooking oil.

One day the village was visited by some young men who called the people together. They said they were students, but at first the farmers could hardly believe it, for they all carried firearms. What kind of scholars were they that meddled with soldiering? As the proverb says : good iron is not used for making nails, good men not for soldiers.

When Lao Ma told of what had happened that day, he always put his hand to the nape of his neck and smiled wistfully. The young men said that the Manchus had been overthrown. It was the Manchus who had forced the Chinese to wear queues. The young men had already cut off their queues, and every true son of China must do the same now that the Chinese had gained their freedom.

Lao Ma was one of the first ones to have his queue cut off. In a way he was sorry to lose it, it was like a part of him, but of course it was the only thing to do. After all, the young men were scholars.

They also said that one should no longer bind the feet of the little girls, but many familes went on doing this. How could a father hope to marry off his daughter if she had feet like a man? More than twenty years were to pass before this custom died out in the country.

When the young men had left, the farmers returned to their ploughing. Freedom—what was that?

" Freedom meant soldiers," Lao Ma said with a wry smile. " Soldiers who plundered and devastated now that there was no emperor to keep them in check, and generals who fought among themselves and divided up the country." The farmers were dragged away to serve under the generals. Lao Ma was lucky enough to escape. Each time an army came to catch recruits, he would run away from his cottage. Once he hid in the stable of the Yao family. A soldier went in to search, but he did not see Lao Ma.

" So it can have its advantages to look like a horse," Lao Ma invariably concluded this story, and the remark was always greeted with a roar of laughter.

Every general had to have grain for his soldiers. They taxed the land and the houses—even the doors and windows. If you could not pay with grain or silver you had to sell your daughters or—if it came to the worst—your land. The land belonged to the family, to the past generations as well as the coming ones. To sell it would be almost a sacrilege.

In those days, the Wang and the Yao families kept increasing their land. Lao Ma somehow managed to hold on to the little piece that was his. " It is a pity that bitterness cannot satisfy the stomach," he said, " for I had to eat a lot of it."

Nobody repaired the dikes any more, so the river would overflow every second or third year. When a harvest was ruined, Lao Ma had to go to the city and pull a rickshaw. Thanks to his strong legs he could run for hours at a stretch. When he came home after a month in the city, he was so thin that his wife turned away her face to hide her tears.

Three of their children died in infancy. During the big cholera epidemic they lost two more, but Lao Ma did not complain. He still had two, and one of them was a son. He did not look like his father—he had his mother's round and mild face and quiet ways.

Two years after the cholera epidemic, the district was afflicted with grasshoppers. They came in a big, dark cloud— it was weird, for they hardly made a sound until they started eating. Then you could hear their crunching from far away. The harvest was just ripening. At first the farmers fought the hungry insects—they hit them with sticks, trampled on them, but it was like battling nature herself.

" So we ate them," Lao Ma said. " When they had devoured our food, we devoured them."

The following year was the year of the big drought. That

Fabulous dog on guard at the entrance of the temple.

The Bund in Shanghai – once the beating heart of the city.

was what finally got Lao Ma down. Both crops withered away before the grain could ripen, and the vegetables never grew more than a couple of inches above the ground. Hungry farmers flocked to the towns and underbid each other to get work. A rickshaw coolie made so little that he himself could hardly live on it.

Even Lao Ma found it hard to smile when he told about the day he went to the Yao family and sold his land. He negotiated with the eldest of the Yao brothers who had just taken over the farm after the death of the head of the family. Lao Ma still remembered how the cup of tea which Yao offered him had made him dizzy—he had not eaten for two days.

When a man is in such straits it is easy to drive a good bargain with him, but young Yao was not like that. He paid a reasonable price for the land. Lao Ma could pay off his debt and had enough left over to keep the wolf from the door until the next harvest.

Now he was landless—he did not even own the earth under his house. When it was sowing time again he became a tenant farmer for Yao, who took two-fifths of the harvest. That was the saddest spring ploughing Lao Ma had ever done, with borrow plough and rented bullock.

When Chiang Kai-shek came to power, times at first improved a little for the villagers. Now there was only one tax collector, but the dikes were still neglected. Man had given up controlling the river—it came and went at will. Some farmers hardly bothered to repair their homes after a flood. What was the use? The river was sure to come back, it always did.

During the early part of the Japanese invasion the village almost became a battlefield. For two days you could hear the thunder of the big guns. Then the troops of Chiang Kai-shek withdrew—after blowing up the big dike. The masses of water halted the Japanese advance for a while, but the spring harvest which had been so promising that year rotted in the fields and many, many people were drowned.

The Japanese were hard masters. When the farmers wailed that they could deliver no more grain, they had to keep some

F

for themselves for the winter, they tasted the boot or the bayonet of the conquerors.

"But the little Japs were easier to deceive than our own officials," Lao Ma said with a wink. "They did not know our hiding places."

For two winters there was such a shortage of fuel that Lao Ma and his family could not have a fire burning under the big *kang*; they froze on the cold bricks. They seldom had more than one meal a day, and even then they could not eat their fill. It was small comfort to hear that conditions were even worse on the other side of the river. Here the plight of the farmers was so great that they even resorted to eating the flesh of the dead.

Everybody longed for the defeat of the Japanese—but when it came it did not better the lives of the farmers. The rich Wang immediately allied himself with the Chiang Kai-shek tax collectors, who were even more greedy after the lean years in the interior. Wang knew where the farmers hid the grain which they needed to keep alive during the winter. He betrayed them to the officials, who confiscated the grain and had the owners whipped.

Money was worth less and less. "That was one good thing for a poor man," said Lao Ma, who used the opportunity to settle a small debt with the Yao family. But when other farmers wanted to pay off their debts to Wang with the now almost worthless paper money, he refused to accept anything but silver.

One day a member of the Yao family showed up in the village. Tai Cheng, was his name. That means *Great Results,* but he had not fulfilled the fond expectations of his parents— on the contrary. Several years ago he had been kicked out of his home. It was rumoured that he had been dishonest in money matters, but no one knew for sure. Such things were kept within the family.

Tai Cheng had experienced much since he left home. At first he was a soldier, then a petty officer in the army of Chiang Kai-shek. He was captured by the Communists and had spent the last four years with them.

The Communists—who were they? The villagers had only heard of red bandits who raped women and killed people who owned anything. Tai Cheng now told them that the Communists were the friends of the poor. " They take the land from the rich and give it to the landless."

He looked with hate towards the home which was closed to him. " They will soon have to pay for their evil deeds," he said. " It will not be long before the Communists come—the Red Army is already on its way."

During the following days his words were often repeated by the villagers—they take the land from the rich and give it to the landless. . . . It sounded too good to be true. No one had ever done anything for the poor. Why should the Communists be an exception?

Some of Chiang Kai-shek's soldiers passed through the village on their retreat to the south. The last thing they did was to go from house to house and collect everything of value. It was not very much—bundles of worn clothes, an old fur coat, a few silver heirlooms. They loaded it on a cart and left.

" May heaven punish them!" shouted a farmer when the last soldier was out of sight. Now the villagers gave vent to their pent-up bitterness—they tried to outdo each other in cursing the ancestors and descendants of the soldiers. Lao Ma won easily, and then they returned to their cold huts and empty larders.

Three days later the first Communists came—a company of soldiers who only stayed overnight before continuing their march southward in pursuit of Chiang Kai-shek's forces. The soldiers were so polite that the farmers could hardly believe their eyes. They asked for permission to billet in the farmhouses and did not steal anything—not that there was much left to steal. They even paid for the little food which the villagers succeeded in scraping together for them. And before they left the next morning, their commander made a speech, thanking the farmers for their hospitality.

Several weeks passed. Lao Ma and his son ploughed the field which had once been theirs; each year they rented the same plot of land from the Yao family. But this year there were no bullocks to be had; they had to pull the plough themselves while Lao Ma's daughter-in-law walked behind and steered. Their sweat watered the earth, and every half hour or so they had to stop and rest.

One morning three young men came to the village. At first they reminded Lao Ma of the scholars who had cut off his queue so many years ago—the newcomers were also armed, and they used strange expressions which the farmers could not understand. They addressed everyone as *Tung Chih*—comrade—and told the farmers to address them the same way.

Tai Cheng must have told the truth, for the three young Communists seemed to be most concerned about the poor. They gathered all the landless farmers and those who had very little land—one of them possessed only a plot that was eight by ten yards. Lao Ma, who was also there, had to answer countless questions. The other farmers were not good at expressing themselves; they preferred Lao Ma to do the talking.

The people kept staring at a shiny object which one of the young men took from his pocket; a pen with its own ink. The pen seemed to fly up and down the paper, for practically everything they said was written down. The young men also wanted to hear about the Wang and Yao families. How much land did they have, and how had they obtained it?

Lao Ma and his son did not attend the last two meetings, they could not neglect the field, but one day all the villagers were called together. They nudged each other and whispered when old Wang came. He had kept indoors lately; he was pale and his hands shook.

One of the young Communists made a speech. The farmers kept looking at the ground as he spoke; some of them picked their teeth or noses. They were embarrassed by all these strange words—freedom, peoples' government, justice. Their minds wandered. It was spring—they would have to tread the water-mill soon . . .

But now the young man said something which caught their attention: "Those who have oppressed the people will be punished. . . . Their land will be taken away from them and given back to the people. . . . Money that is owed to them will not have to be paid back. . . . Let everyone step forward who has something to complain about."

After a moment of silence, a young farmer by name of Li stood up. He said that once he had his own land, but then his father died and he had to borrow money for the funeral. The debt increased, they took the land away from him . . .

" Who are *they*?" interrupted the young man.

Li muttered something.

" Speak up, so that everyone can hear !"

" It was Mr. Wang . . ." Instinctively, Li had used the polite term of address. Everybody avoided looking at Wang— it was embarrassing to talk in this way about a man who was present. But the young Communist turned and pointed at Wang.

" *Mr.*, you call him ! He is not that, nor is he our comrade —he is an enemy of the people ! Don't you understand ? For years he has robbed and exploited you ! Why all this respect ? Stand up and speak your bitterness !"

Another farmer rose, then two more. Old Chu told how the Chiang Kai-shek gendarmes had taken away his only son —at that time, Wang had been the local recruiting agent for the army, and Chu had been unable to pay the fifty dollars which Wang had demanded to let his son go free. The son never came back. Another said that he had lost his wife because Wang had told the officials where he had hid the family's supply of grain—that winter they starved, when she died she was only a skeleton.

" You demanded extortionate interest !" " You took my land !" " You cheated me !" They came close to Wang and pointed at him, shook their fists in front of his face. Their voices rose—their anger was like the river water when it finally breaks through the dikes.

" We all agree on Wang's guilt." Again it was the young man with the shiny pen who spoke. " But is he the only enemy of the people ? Are there no other rich men who have been exploiters of the poor ?"

Everybody looked at Yao, but no one said anything. Then Tai Cheng rose and walked slowly towards the old man. His words sent a shiver through all of them. A son accusing his father—the ancestors must turn in their graves!

Tai Cheng declared that his father had also exploited the poor. He spoke shrilly. Lao Ma hardly dared to look at Yao. The old man was white in the face, but he did not flinch.

" It isn't true!" Without realizing it, Lao Ma had jumped to his feet. " He has not cheated us! He bought my land when I was in need, but he paid a reasonable price for it!"

" Why did he grow wealthy while everyone else was suffering?" one of the young Communists demanded. " Why did he live in luxury while others starved? It is the rich who have exploited and tormented you . . ."

There was a murmur of agreement. All restraint seemed to have disappeared after Tai Cheng had spoken against his father. The farmers were still pointing and shouting at Wang and Yao, but it was really no longer those two men whom they attacked—it was their own miserable existence, the endless fight for food, the hopeless struggle against the river.

" Have these two evil enemies of the people ever shown pity for the victims?" the young man asked.

" No, no!"

" Do they not deserve death?"

" Yes—kill them *sha, sha*!"

" It is the will of the people," said the young Communist. The two men had their arms tied and were led away. Lao Ma stayed behind. " *Sha, sha*!"—the shouts became fainter and fainter. A while later he heard two shots. He gave a start. He thought of old Yao. Then he thought of the land he had lost. Soon it would again be his.

CHAPTER X

The New Gods

LAO MA HEARD footsteps outside the hut. A shadow moved across the paper window, and a moment later the door was torn open. It was the neighbour's youngest son.

" There is going to be a meeting at sunset—it is very important."

Another meeting, Lao Ma thought, but he checked himself. " Good, good," he said. " I will be there."

The door was slammed shut. Lao Ma shook his head. That boy was not turning out very well. He talked to grown-ups as if he were their equal, and last New Year he had refused to kowtow to his parents.

But what could one expect? At a meeting some time ago, the boy had complained because his father had struck him. And young Li, the head of the farmers' association, had agreed with the lad although Lao Ma had thought that it was a well-deserved box on the ear. After all, one could not permit the children to disobey and to answer back.

But Lao Ma had not said anything at the meeting. He sat in silence while young Li reproached his neighbour. People should no longer chastize their children, Li said, for in New China all were equal, young and old. Lao Ma sniffed contemptuously. As if age and experience did not mean anything. But nowadays the children were treated as if they were the ancestors themselves . . .

He took a bottle from the *kang*. Carefully he poured a little water into the washbasin—nice, warm water that sent a cloud of steam up into the air. It was a wonderful bottle. If you filled it with boiling water in the evening, the water kept hot until the next day. One no longer had to drink cold water when one woke up at night and was thirsty.

Practically everyone in the village now had such a bottle. The washbasin was also new—it was white with a red rim, and at the bottom was a round, smiling child's face. How different from the old clay basins that always broke! In the old days the farmers had not been able to afford such things, but now they sometimes had a little money.

When Lao Ma was through washing himself, he could no longer see the child's face at the bottom of the washbasin. Before throwing the water outside the door, he sprinkled the earthen floor to bind the dust. He put the ball of soap on top of the beam where the rats could not get at it. Then he put on his padded blue jacket. That was the last thing his wife had made for him before she died last year. Many a time she had stroked the material with her bony hands—it was a wonder, she had often said, that almost everyone could now afford to have new clothes.

Was it not wrong after all that she did not get a better funeral? Lao Ma had intended to buy a small paper house that was to be carried in the procession and burned together with the paper money. Even if she had been poor all her life, she ought to have been sent off to the ancestors in a decent fashion. How could one expect her to be well treated if she came as an insignificant person?

But young Li had said that such things did not mean anything any more. Superstition, he had called it. And when Lao Ma went to town anyway to buy the paper money, it turned out that one could not even get it any more. The shop where one had bought such things now sold cloth.

One did not give a funeral feast any more, either—just a modest meal for the closest relatives. In this matter, however, Lao Ma had done what he thought right. He bought a piece of pork and a bottle of wine and treated his relatives.

Young Li was also against old-style weddings, so the villagers no longer carried the bride to the groom's house in a closed sedan chair. To bring her in this way was to signify

that she was the groom's chattel, Li said, and it was also undignified for human beings to carry other human beings. So
now the beautiful red chair was gathering dust.

But it just was not the same, Lao Ma thought, when a bride
came rumbling in a cart and when she and the groom merely
bowed in front of Chairman Mao's picture in the meeting hall.
Lao Ma preferred the old custom where the couple knelt in
front of the ancestral altar after drinking wine from the same
cup. Some of the other villagers probably felt the same way,
but people kept such things to themselves these days. It was not
good to be stamped as old-fashioned and reactionary . . .

When Lao Ma came outside his house he put his hand
through a hole behind the doorpost and bolted the door from
the inside. There was really no reason to do this any more.
One no longer had to worry about vagabonds or rascals sneak-
ing in and stealing while one was out. During the six years
that had passed since Chairman Mao became the leader of
the country, there had not been a single case of theft in the
village.

With the short, hesitant steps of an old man he walked
down the narrow path. The tracks left by his wheelbarrow
were hard as stone after the frost. On his right was the temple,
a low, red stone building, very old. Only once had he seen the
little mirror that was set in the ridge of the roof. That was
when, as a boy, he had climbed the tall tree on the Yao farm.
He could still remember how the mirror had sparkled in the
sunlight. One could very well understand that the evil spirits
became frightened and fled when they came swooping down
from the sky and suddenly saw their own terrible faces in the
mirror . . .

Lao Ma could never walk past the temple without thinking
of the day when the gods were turned out of their home. That
was shortly after the land distribution; the three young Communists had still been here. They had said that the village
needed a school, and everyone agreed with them. Only there
was no house that suited the purpose—it had to be large, for
there were nearly a hundred children in the village.

At first there was talk about using the Wang family's farm,

but it was too far away. The Yao farm had already been made the headquarters of the new farmers' association. When one of the young Communists suggested turning the temple into a school, the farmers hesitated. The young men laughed.

" Have the gods protected you against the river? Have they prevented the rich from exploiting you. Have they kept sickness and starvation from your door?"

No, and the farmers had never had much confidence in the gods. They were distant and impersonal—not like the ancestors whose altar stood in every home. Only with the ancestors was there a strong, personal tie. But even so, would it not be unwise actually to challenge the old gods?

One of the young men said that the gods had only been used to fool the people, they were nothing but painted wooden figures, but everybody knew that the village needed a school. Why not use the temple? It was finally put to a vote—that was the new custom of putting up your hand to show that you agreed with the speaker.

During the voting, the three young men had kept a watchful eye on the people. Who knows—maybe they would remember you if you did not raise your hand. Look, there were already many who had done so—it was probably wiser to follow their example ...

The children had laughed and shouted when the ancient gods were dragged outside and thrown behind the temple— warriors with scarlet faces, executioners whose axes and drawn swords broke like matchsticks. Kwan Yin followed—the wistfully smiling goddess of mercy to whom barren women for countless generations had sacrificed little dolls. And finally came Lung Wang, the Dragon King—He who controlled the sources of the water.

There were probably others besides Lao Ma who had halfway expected a catastrophe the following spring, but the river behaved better than it had done within living memory. The harvest became so bountiful that there was hardly room for it in the granaries. It looked as if the power of the old gods had been broken.

" What do we need them for?" a farmer asked with a laugh

as they were gathering the harvest. "Now we have our own living Buddha—Chairman Mao!"

Lao Ma realized that there were other explanations for the good harvest. Never before had the farmers worked so hard. Those who had no land had only received a small plot each during the land distribution, but now it was *theirs*. Even the birds seemed to sing it when you opened your eyes in the morning—it is your land, it is your land! In those days Lao Ma scarcely had time to swallow the thin gruel and salted turnips that was his breakfast, he was in such a hurry to get out in his field.

After the land distribution, the farmers took turns using the bullocks which had belonged to Wang and Yao. There was occasional disagreement as to who was to feed them, and many thought that the others used them longer than they ought to, but young Li always ironed out the difficulties.

Li had become a big man in the village. Before the three Communists left he was elected chairman of the farmers' association. Everybody knew that the Communists liked him, so they all voted for him—also Lao Ma, although he really did not care for him. Li was too direct. He was able and honest, yes—but Lao Ma thought that he might give other people a little more face.

Shortly after he was elected, Li had gone away for several months—to Peking, at the invitation of the new government. When he returned, he had changed. It was not just the flat, foreign cap that he wore, or his shiny new button with a picture of Chairman Mao. He also spoke differently—used strange words and expressions. *Work-together-in-unison,* he often said, and he pronounced it as if it were one word. When he wanted to recommend something he always described it as *united-front-united-effort* towards *new-strength-unity*. Those who disagreed with him he called *go-against-the-current* obstructionists.

That was what he had called Lao Ma and the two other farmers when they had refused to join the new mutual-aid teams. These teams were organized by the farmers' association —all the farmers worked together, first on one man's land, then on another's. Some thought the work was easier this way.

When the teams were formed, Lao Ma had said that he did not want to join right away, he preferred to wait and see. He quickly added that he realized that the new arrangement would be very advantageous for everyone.

"But I am afraid that it will not be good for the rest of you to have me join. I am an old man. I can no longer keep up with the young people."

What he really meant was quite different. How could one be sure that a man would plough another man's land as thoroughly as he did his own? Would anyone gather somebody else's grain as carefully as he did his own? No—only when a man worked his own land, was he sure to do his best. That was how people were.

Li said that of course it was up to them, only those who wanted to should join the mutual-aid teams. "We do not use force in new China," he said. But since Lao Ma and the two others did not want to co-operate with the rest, they naturally could not expect to enjoy the advantages of the farmers' association . . .

Later, when Lao Ma wanted to borrow the bullocks, it was always difficult to get them. It was the farmers' association which decided who was to use them, and Li was its chairman. And when Lao Ma wanted seed he could not get as much as he needed—it was no longer possible to buy seed except through the farmers' association.

In the end, the three farmers went to Li and said that they wanted to join the mutual-aid teams after all. Li had won, so he ought to have pretended that there had never been any disagreement at all. Instead, he made a long speech about it at the next meeting—rubbed salt into the wounds. He said that Lao Ma and the two others had finally come to realize that it was unwise to go against the current, that it was better to join hands with the people under the leadership of the glorious Communist party and Chairman Mao . . .

On his way to the meeting hall, Lao Ma had come to the new hothouses which stood on a field that had once belonged to Yao. He stopped for a moment and looked at the long rows of paper windows facing south. It was young Li who had suggested that the association build the hothouses. No one could deny that they had been a big success. Formerly, the farmers had little to do during the winter months. Some went to town to find work. Others just sat around and waited for spring. Now each man worked a couple of hours a day in the hothouses, and each family got a handy little sum from the sale of the big, red tomatoes.

Nor could one deny that the land yielded more with the new methods of cultivation. It was young Li who had arranged for farm specialists to come and talk to the villagers. These men had taught them to use the white powder which is almost as effective as human fertilizer. They had also taught them that the yield increases if one uses selected seed, and had shown them how to fight harmful insects.

But most important of all was the fact that the new government had immediately taken up the struggle with the river. At first it was the farmers themselves who did the work—they were directed by people from Peking, just like in the old days. Later came thousands and thousands of men who were guarded by soldiers. The farmers were not allowed to talk to them; they were only told that these prisoners were enemies of the people.

The dikes grew rapidly, but during the third year after Chairman Mao had become leader of the country, the river decided to show that it was still master. In two days the water rose over twenty feet, and although every man was called to the dikes, the river broke through. For three weeks the water was ankle-deep in Lao Ma's hut. Grain and vegetables rotted in the fields.

A few of the farmers were of the thrifty type—they were the ones who had had their own land even before the land distribution. They had a stock of grain and thus had nothing to fear, but many of the others became panicky. How were they going to live until the next harvest? Nobody could lend them money now that Wang and Yao were dead. To go to the town was no use—it was nearly impossible to find a job, and begging was now prohibited.

Young Li promised that a way out would be found, but not many believed him. Some of the villagers sold part of their land to those who were better off; they were paid in grain.

How they regretted it when the horse-carts came and sack after sack of grain was unloaded and distributed among the farmers! "But we cannot pay for it," a old man said. "You don't have to," came the answer. "It is from the government."

Afterwards young Li had made a speech which the villagers would never forget. In the old days it was every man for himself, he said, but the new government had taught them the strength of unity. Now the villagers were no longer alone in their struggle against the river. Behind them stood the whole nation, lead by Chairman Mao. They would never have to live in fear of famine any more, for if the harvest failed in one place, the government would send grain from another place where the harvest had been good.

In the end he had said that this would undoubtedly be the last flood. The government was making a big lake further up the river. If there was too much water it would just flow into this lake which was so large that it could never overflow . . .

Lao Ma had not heard the rest. He just sat there, getting used to this strange new thought;; you no longer have to fear the river. It no longer controls our lives—it is we who are masters . . .

About half a year after the flood, Li had suggested that the farmers' association be given greater power. He wanted it to decide what each farmer should grow, and to take over the harvest and dispose of it. The association would then see to it that the government got its share of the grain as tax—usually one-fifth of the harvest.

The new arrangement meant that the individual farmer could no longer bring his produce to the market and sell it himself. This meant a loss to the farmers, as the prices on the " free " market were higher than those paid by the government. Even so, they agreed to it without much hesitation, for Li made it clear to them that the government needed the grain. The government had helped them when they were in need—

now it was their turn to help the government. That was only fair.

But then Li came with his suggestion about removing the fences between the fields—that was just after Lao Ma had buried his wife. He remembered it clearly, for the family had still been wearing white cloth on their shoes for mourning. He also remembered the icy silence which had followed Li's words.

And Li had spoken faster and faster, for he could feel that this time no one was with him. All over China, he had said, the farmers were demanding *increased socialization*—more of his fine phrases. Nothing could stop the peoples' march towards the *common-ownership-future* which was the goal of the government and the nation. Did the people of this village want to be the only ones who resisted the new idea?

" Why should the fences be removed?"

The question came from a young farmer. At the land distribution he had become owner of a piece of land, for the first time in his life. Now he feared that they wanted to take it away from him again.

" It is more practical," Li had replied. " Now you have to turn the plough so often—that will not be necessary when it becomes one big field."

" We don't mind turning the plough so often."

" In a few years we will get tractors which can pull the plough," Li had continued. " If there are fences, we will not be able to use the tractors."

" Then let us wait until we get the tractors!"

" We are doing well now, why make changes?"

For a moment Li had seemed at a loss. He took out a letter which he had received from the authorities. His eyes ran up and down the lines—many of the farmers had learned to read in the association, but he could read faster than anyone else in the village.

" There is strength in unity," he then said. " The new idea, which has sprung from the people, will lead to greater unity, greater strength . . ."

" I want to keep my land!"

Li looked up quickly. He was not used to being interrupted.
" But you *will* keep it !"

" Why then remove the fences?"

" Because . . . " He explained that nothing was being taken away from them. They would only own the land in common—collectively. In this way they would all have greater security. As it was now, a man could be ruined by one bad harvest. He would no longer run such a risk. Besides, some farmers had already sold part of the land which had been given them—a dangerous thing, for in this way a new class of landless and a class of landowners would again come into being. That would be prevented if the land became common property. Then the whole village would become like one big family that shared everything . . .

" But why?" they had asked. " Why should we do it when we will rather not?"

Li had fingered the shiny button which had been given him in Peking.

" Nobody *has* to," he had said. " The people's government never uses force. It is the people's friend. But it has no patience with those who only think of themselves—the enemies of the people."

It was as if you could hear the last words long after he had said them. Lao Ma was sure that many of the others also had thought of Wang and Yao at that moment. *Enemies of the people*—that was what they had been called . . .

Li went on talking. When the *common-ownership* plan became a fact, accounts would be made after each harvest. So and so much grain would go to the government, so and so much would be put aside as a reserve, and the rest would be divided among them all according to how much each one had worked. Those who worked longer would get more. The lazy would have to manage with less. Your income would no longer depend on how much land you owned, or whether you were lucky with the harvest, but on how hard you worked . . .

Then we will not be farmers any more, Lao Ma thought—we will be like the labourers in the town.

Peasants bringing their wares to "the free market" in town.

Green vegetables being pitted for the winter – everything is now done collectively.

When the new plan came to a vote, Li had smiled with satis-
faction. There was not one who had not raised his hand.

That evening Lao Ma had gone out in the field and picked
up a lump of earth. For many years it had belonged to his
family. Then he lost it, got it back—and now they would take
it away from him again. The earth crumbled between his
fingers, he stood empty-handed in the dark night . . .

That was nearly a year ago. There had been many meetings
since then—about cleanliness and improved agricultural
methods, and there had also been talks by people who spoke
about women's rights and such things. One did learn something from these meetings, only there were too many of them.
One got so tired—after all, he was getting to be an old man.
True, nobody said that one *had* to go, but it would look strange
if one stayed at home . . .

Tonight's meeting was also a very important one, the neighbour's son had said. Lao Ma looked up—his mind had wandered, he had forgotten the time. The sun had already set
and it was getting dark. He walked faster; when he
entered the meeting hall he was out of breath. The big table
was still there—the same one he and Yao had sat at when they
negotiated about the land. Now young Li was standing at the
table. He had just begun to talk.

Li said that he had been seriously reprimanded by Peking.
The village had not fulfilled its *quota*—that was another new
word which was often used. You had to do so much work each
hour, each day and each month—otherwise you did not fulfil
your quota, and that was very bad. There was a quota for each
village, for each province and one for all China—but that was
so big that a farmer could not grasp the figures.

The fields were not so well taken care of as before, Li continued. He said that this was due to *those who went against
the current*. They pretended to be friends of the people, but in
reality they were striving to undermine the efforts of the
government . . .

Lao Ma suppressed a smile. Did Li really believe what he
had just said? Did he not realize that no one in the village
was hostile towards the new government? The fact that they

G

did not take as much pains as before was due to quite different reasons. A woman did not take as good care of other people's children as she did of her own. A man did not till other people's fields as well as his own.

That was why they did not plough as deeply or weed as thoroughly as before. That was why more grain was lost when they gleaned the fields at harvest time, and why the men did not pedal as hard on the treadmill. When you saw others shirk, you did likewise.

About half a year ago the government had allotted each farmer a small plot, forty by forty feet. These plots were cultivated much more thoroughly than the common fields, Li continued.

Yes, Lao Ma thought, for that is our own land. What we grow there we do not have to share wth others.

The farmers would have found it hard make ends meet if they had not put so much work into the " private field," as they called it. The government took away more and more of what was grown on the common land. This year the farmers had been allowed to keep only three hundred pounds of grain for each member of the family. Lao Ma had heard that the city-dwellers got even less grain, it was rationed, but then they could buy meat and cakes and such things. The villagers had practically nothing but the grain, and it was not enough. Nobody ate more than two meals a day, and one meal was usually thin porridge.

In the spring and summer months, when the farmers worked hard, they usually ate more than their ration. Then they had to tighten their belts even more in the winter. Often they got nothing but potatoes. They had been told to grow a lot of potatoes—it paid better than most other plants, Li had said— but the farmers detested potatoes. They just did not seem to fill your stomach properly.

And that is all I will get tonight, Lao Ma thought with disgust. There was not even a little oil to fry them in—at least that gave them some taste. The ration of oil had become smaller and smaller during the last few years—now each farmer got only a tiny cup a month. One could not get *dofu*, either—all the soyabeans had to be handed over to the government.

Li had often explained to them that they were not tightening their belts in vain. It was for the benefit of the whole nation—the products which the government took over were used to pay for machines which would produce goods for all of them. But that did not help the gnawing in one's stomach—at times it was almost as bad as during a famine in the old days.

The farmers occasionally had a little ready cash now—despite the decline in production after the fields had become common property, the land still yielded more than before. There was also the income from the hothouses, and some farmers went to town and sold the produce of their private plots.

But what was the use of money? One could buy washbasins and metal pots and such things, but food was what the farmers needed most of all, and that they could not buy. At New Year, some of them had gone to town and bought unrationed food-stuffs. On the way back, however, they were stopped by police-men. They were very kind, but they had confiscated the food-stuffs, explaining that it was not permitted to take food from the city to the country . . .

How sombre Li's face was compared to Chairman Mao's smiling picture on the wall! Li exhorted them to pull them-selves together, to make greater effort. He reminded them of how much they owed the government. Had it not chased away Chiang Kai-shek and the evil landlords? Did it not teach their children to read and write? Did they not wear better clothes than before?

The farmers nodded automatically after each question. They had heard it all so many times before. Lao Ma's atten-tion was caught by a spider which hung down from the ceiling just above Li's head. Each time it was about to touch Li, it would climb up again a little. How clearly I can see the spider, Lao Ma mused. When things were close to his eyes they often blurred, but at a distance all the details stood out . . .

" . . . And have we not broken the power of the river?" came Li's voice. Lao Ma forgot the spider. He nodded enthusiastically—yes, they had tamed the river. His grandsons and their children again would grow up without the fear of the old enemy ...

Lao Ma smiled, and for a moment he even forgot that he was going to have boiled potatoes for dinner.

CHAPTER XI

The Mandate Of Heaven

MAC AND I met on the border between Hong Kong and China. We were both on our way to Peking by the same train. I immediately took a liking to the big, friendly Britisher who was so charmingly boyish despite his white hair. But when I heard that he was a journalist, my face fell.

And so did Mac's. We had both hoped to be the only foreign correspondent in China—then the stories would be more exclusive. We soon agreed, though, that we did not have to get into each other's hair. China was big enough for two of us.

When we got off the train in Peking, we solemnly shook hand and wished each other good luck.

A few days later, I had an appointment with the vice-president of the Democratic Women's League. Long before I entered the room I could hear Mac's booming voice. At factories or on collective farms, in schools and at a home for the deaf-and-dumb—everywhere I went during the next few weeks I saw Mac's white mane, or else he had just been there.

It was no coincidence that our paths crossed to often. When a foreign correspondent in Red China wants to make an interview or to visit some place, he must first go to the Foreign Office. Here they also help him with suggestions about where he can find material.

But the ministry has most practice in handing big delegations, and of course it prefers to kill as many birds as possible with one stone. It has a large and varied itinerary which foreign visitors can choose from. Do you want to know about religion in China? A Buddhist monk or a Catholic priest—both leftists, of course—are immediately put at your disposal.

You can also talk to a former gangster leader who now devotes his life to the new welfare state, or an ex-capitalist who preaches socialism. You are kindly received everywhere, but once in a while you get a feeling that the people you talk to are thinking about something else—they somehow remind you of actors who know their roles too well.

One day I was to meet Mr. Sao, the leader of China's Democratic League—China is the only iron-curtain country which permits other parties besides the Communist. The appointment was for eleven o'clock, but I came about ten minutes before the appointed time. Mr. Sao is also early, I thought, seeing a hat and coat in the corridor.

I opened the door—and guess who was standing in the middle of the room, grinning broadly?

" Well, I guess China isn't big enough after all," Mac said, adding that it might turn out to be an interesting interview. Mr. Sao was supposed to be able to prove that new China really is much more democratic than the western countries.

Yes, so I had heard. I sat down in one of the huge plush sofas and looked around. On the wall opposite me hung a mirror in an ornate golden frame, and from the polished bureau below a stuffed bird glared maliciously at me.

Why do modern Chinese have such a taste in furniture? Few people have a richer inheritance to choose from—but they seem to prefer Europe's Victorian taste. It seems to me that the Japanese have the most beautiful homes in the world, whereas most better-class Chinese homes remind me of pretentious European boarding houses. Why this big difference between the two neighbours?

" In China we held on to the old ways as long as we possibly could," Chi-yun once explained to me. " We believed that our own culture was superior to all others. Suddenly we discovered that the West was ahead of us in many ways. Those of us who wanted to be modern decided that our old ways were no use any more, so we swept aside everything Chinese."

The Japanese, on the other hand, only imitated the technique of the west. In their homes, they preserved their own taste and traditions. Their clothing and furniture, as well as most of their customs, were copied from China more than a thousand years ago. Thus it happens that the simple, æsthetic taste of ancient China still lives on in Japan, but not—at least for the moment—in its original homeland . . .

"Here he comes." Mac rose. The door was opened and a bespectacled Chinese entered, followed by a young woman.

One could tell right away that Mr. Sao was a southerner. They are usually slight and have very little hair on their faces. Their skin is fine and light-coloured. They seem almost feminine compared to the big northerners who, during the centuries, have become mixed with Tartars, Mongols and other primitive peoples. The northerners are usually more naïve and crude than the southerners.

Mac bowed. "It is a pleasure for me to meet the leader of the opposition."

Mr. Sao looked startled. "There must be a misunderstanding," he said. "There is no opposition in China."

It was Mac's turn to look startled. "But then what's the purpose of your party?"

Mr. Sao smiled and sipped his tea. Then he began to explain how democracy functions in new China.

"From the people, to the people," is one of Mao Tse-tung's favourite slogans. The Communists maintain that everything good and beautiful originates with the broad, toiling masses. As the masses find it difficult to express themselves, the Communists help them—they listen to the wishes of the people and carry them out.

The most important sounding-boards are the street and village committees. You find them in every inhabited place throughout the enormous country. Here the people can voice their opinions at regular meetings. These opinions are forwarded to the National Assembly in Peking, a kind of Congress or House of Commons. Some of the suggestions of the people become decrees or laws which are then explained at the village or street committee meetings.

From the people, to the people—the circle is complete.

"But how . . ." Before Mac could get any further Mr. Sao

raised his hand. He wanted to finish talking before we began questioning him.

Of course it is not easy for the Communists to listen to all the Chinese, he continued—there are so many of them. The Communists have therefore permitted the existence of about half a dozen other parties which are supposed to help them. Mr. Sao's party represented the intellectuals.

" All the members of my party agree that socialism is the best system for China," Mr. Sao told us. The new constitution states this in any case. " But many of our members do not have much contact with the Communists. They prefer to express their opinions through their own party."

Many other organizations assist the Communists in the same way—unions, women's clubs, youth leagues, and a Sino-Soviet Friendship Association. This last association alone has more than fifty million members. The army and navy of Red China were enrolled at one stroke—an act that makes me think of Feng Yu-hsiang, the famous Christian General from the days of the war-lords. Feng had his entire army baptised in one day with a firehose . . .

Mr. Sao also told us how elections are held in new China. First there are consultations between the parties for the purpose of nominating candidates. " These consultations take place in a spirit of friendship and mutual confidence," Mr. Sao said. Those who are most " progressive " are preferred, although they do not have to be members of the Communist party.

The candidates are then introduced to the street and village committees of their districts. Anyone can question or criticize them. They are finally approved by all the members, as usual by a show of hands. Then the election begins . . .

" But why . . ." Mac tried again to break in, but Mr. Sao continued unperturbed. During elections in the so-called democratic countries, he said—and he was referring to us, the western democracies—it is money that counts. The party that spends the most on the election campaign will win. This is not so in China, where no money is spent on propaganda during elections. The list of candidates is merely sent around to the voters, who sign it. If they cannot write they leave a thumb-print.

"But is the list always approved by the voters?" Mac had finally managed to get a word in.

"Yes, of course."

"But what if there's a candidate you don't like?"

"Then you just cross out his name and put somebody else's name instead."

"Does that ever happen?"

"Not that I know of. If you have any objection to a candidate, all you have to do is to say so when he is introduced at a street or village committee meeting."

"I see," Mac said despairingly. "But there is just one thing I understand. Everything seems to be decided beforehand, so why go to the trouble of holding the election?"

Mr. Sao adjusted his glasses. "Because . . ." He cleared his throat. "Because it is democratic."

Mac and I glanced at each other. Then I said that I would like to hear some more about the street committees. The leaders of these committees are almost invariably progressives, and the meetings always end with unanimous acceptance of whatever the leader proposes.

"Could that be because the leaders sometimes lock the door and say that they won't open it again until everybody agrees?"

"I have heard of such cases." Mr. Sao shook his head. "But it is incorrect to act like that, it is not democratic."

He must have felt that his personal experiences with Chinese democracy would seem more convincing to us, for now he began to tell us about himself. He had founded the Democratic League many years ago, when Chiang Kai-shek was in power. In those days he had his own newspaper, but it was banned every time he dared to criticize the government. He finally moved to Hong Kong, where he could express himself freely under British protection.

When the Japanese attacked Hong Kong he returned to China. Towards the end of the war, several prominent members of his party were murdered by Chiang's secret police. They had dared to say publicly what every Chinese knew in his heart—that Chiang's government was corrupt and did not work for the people, only for itself.

" Now we have an honest government which really does something for the people," Mr. Sao continued enthusiastically, and I felt sure that he meant what he was saying. " The Communists have shown confidence in us. Many of our members have been entrusted with high positions. The new government listens to our advice . . ."

I thought of my mother-in-law. She is a very public-spirited woman; for years she has supported various charity organizations. When the Communists came to power, this kind of work was taken over by the state. She was a widow now; her children had left her and she felt lonely and useless.

" Nobody has any use for an old woman like me," she wrote to us.

But shortly after our arrival in Peking she received an invitation from a committee which advised the government on welfare work in the capital. She was invited to the committee's next meeting. When she left she was not very enthusiastic— she figured that she would merely have to listen to the reading of some reports. When she came home that evening, however, she was in a wonderful mood.

" Everybody was invited to speak," she said. " Of course I didn't think they would care to hear my opinion, but they insisted that I also express my views. Afterwards they said that my suggestions were very sensible. And imagine, Chi-yun, I was elected to a special committee of inspection—your old mother isn't so useless after all ! "

Mr. Sao also felt that he was of use to new China. That was why he and his party co-operated with the government. Mac and I tried to find out how great power the non-Communist parties have. Mr. Sao replied that all the parties have representatives in the National Congress.

" But do these parties have any influence on the national policy ?"

" To a certain extent."

Could he give us a concrete example ?

Mr. Sao hesitated. " Some professors recently complained that they had to attend too many political meetings, it interfered with their work. We brought this to the attention of the government. Now the professors only have to attend important meetings."

Mac and I looked up from our notebooks in surprise.

" Couldn't you give us an—uh—a slightly more striking example?" Mac asked. Not offhand, Mr. Sao replied, but he repeated that the government always pays attention to the suggestions of the small parties. " And that is more than Chiang Kai-shek ever did," he concluded.

We nodded. The good points of the Communists stood out clearly, especially if one compared them to Chiang. But it seemed to us that there was one thing lacking in new China— individual freedom.

I have heard Communists say that the people has unlimited freedom under Mao Tse-tung. Mr. Sao was wiser than that, however. He hinted politely that it would be worth while for us to study the background of the revolution a little. If we looked into China's past, he said, we might understand why individual freedom was not valued very highly in his country.

Mac and Mr. Sao now began discussing the meaning of such words as freedom and democracy. My mind began to wander. Wasn't there something to what Mr. Sao had said? I thought of China's long history ...

At the time when the Roman Empire was born, China became united under one emperor. Until then the country had consisted of several kingdoms, each one under a highly centralized government. De-centralized governments would not have been able to fight the ever-present danger of floods.

Confucius spent most of his days travelling and preaching charity and justice to rulers who listened willingly enough to the great humanist. But this did not prevent them from ruling harshly. Again and again, Chinese history tells us about men who were exiled or castrated as punishment for slight offences against the throne. In more serious cases, not only the sinner but his whole family were executed. To hold the clan responsible for the actions of the individual was an old Chinese custom.

The people found nothing unnatural in these cruel punishments. It was the duty of the subjects to be loyal to the emperor. His mandate to rule came from heaven. The people owed him blind obedience—as long as he ruled well.

But no further. The history of China is full of bloody rebellions. The purpose was never to abolish the throne, however. That would have been high treason. No, the rebels only wanted to depose a ruler who had become corrupt and incompetent, thus making himself unworthy of the mandate of heaven.

The rebellions usually took place when a dynasty had ruled for many years and become degenerate. If there were too many floods because the dikes were not kept in repair, or if taxes became unbearably heavy—then the flag of rebellion would be raised, and it was not lowered until a better ruler sat on the throne.

In Europe we have often fought for freedom. The Chinese have not, with the exception of the 1911 revolution against the Manchus and the rebellion against the barbarous Mongols in 1367. Both were non-Chinese dynasties.

When the Mongols conquered China in the thirteen century it infuriated them to find only towns and agricultural land, but no pastures for their horses. Many of the Mongols were in favour of killing off the population, razing the cities and letting the grass grow, but this was fortunately prevented by one of Gengis Khan's advisers. He told the great khan that it would be unwise to kill the goose that lays the golden eggs.

About a century later, rebellions began to weaken the Mongols' grip on China. The Mongols had made a serious mistake by not using Chinese officials in the administration, thus making enemies of the intellectuals.

The root of the trouble was that there were too many Chinese, declared one of the khan's ministers. He proposed killing off all Chinese by the name of Chang, Wang, Liu, Li and Chao—that would have been like exterminating all English people with the names of Jones, Smith, Green, White and

Johnson. But before this plan could be carried out the Mongols were overthrown.

Towards the end of Europe's Middle Age, rebellions became more and more frequent in China. This was mainly due to population pressure. No more land was to be had in the south-western provinces which had hitherto been able to absorb the surplus population. The provinces along the coast had to feed more and more mouths.

To survive, the farmers started home industries, weaving cloths and making utensils which they sold in the towns. This helped a little, but then came the western nations and Japan and forced China to buy their cheap industrial products. The farmers could not compete. The suffering in the country increased—and so did the number of attempted revolutions.

Two of these rebellions resulted in the loss of millions of lives. During the middle of the last century, south China rose under a Christian leader who called his movement *Tai Ping*—the Great Peace. Ten years passed before the Manchus, aided by the Christian foreign powers, were able to suppress the rebels.

In the beginning of this century, large parts of north China were overrun by revolutionaries whom the Europeans called the Boxers. The rebels first wanted to overthrow the Manchus, but the sly empress succeeded in turning their wrath against the foreign powers which had forced the weakened Manchus to give them concessions. The representatives of the foreign powers were besieged in the legation quarter in Peking. Only when European and Japanese troops arrived were the rebels subdued.

Many thought that the Taiping rebellion was a religious movement and that the Boxer rebellion was caused by the anti-foreign feelings among the Chinese. In both cases, the explosions were really caused by the dissatisfaction of the farmers.

In 1911 the imperial throne was overthrown. To do so proved surprisingly easy—because the discontent in the country was greater than ever. Most Chinese expected another dynasty to succeed the Manchus. Any dynasty that had made a sincere attempt to relieve the suffering in the country by somehow solving the farm problem, would most likely have become popular. But the leaders of the revolution belonged to the upper classes. They were idealists who understood little of China's real problems. Dr. Sun Yat-sen, who headed the revolution, had spent most of his life as a political refugee in Japan, England or the U.S.A. He wanted to make China a democracy in the western pattern.

The attempt was a fiasco from the very beginning. When the throne toppled, it was as if the moral standards of the Chinese went with it. The Chinese have always had a strong sense of loyalty, but who was there now to be loyal to? The revolutionaries? They did their best to wipe out the old traditions, but the new ideas which they tried to replant from foreign countries did not take root in China. The " modern " Chinese, who spoke so loudly about democracy and freedom, were seldom shining examples to others. The " new individualism " often meant avoiding the clan responsibility without replacing it with a new sense of responsibility towards society as a whole. Or should one be loyal to the warlords who quickly saw their chance to seize power?

For thousands of years the Chinese have called their country *The Middle Kingdom*—the centre of the world. There is pride in that name, but now they were ashamed because China was weak and looked down upon. England and Japan behaved as if they were masters of the country. In the large cities along the coast, factories were springing up, accompanied by the usual misery and suffering of an industrial revolution. Starving farmers who flocked to the towns were brutally exploited by the new capitalists. Millions starved to death after a big flood or drought without anyone raising a finger to help them.

When Chiang Kai-shek defeated the warlords and united the country he was greeted with enthusiasm. Here was finally a strong man who could bring law and order and make China respected again. It soon turned out, though, that he was more of a politician than a statesman. His main concern was to preserve his own power.

Chiang lost his " mandate of heaven " because he did nothing for the farmers who make up eighty per cent of the population of China. The dissatisfaction of the farmers was the driving power behind Mao Tse-tung's victory.

Now the civil war is finally over. Today the Chinese have what they missed most of all—a strong government. This government has taken over the responsibilities towards the people of the old imperial government. That it is a Communist government does not matter much to the Chinese. They have never been interested in politics. They feel that they owe the new government their loyalty as long as it rules well . . .

I looked at Mr. Sao, who was still discussing democracy with Mac—they did not seem to be getting anywhere. The Chinese do not miss personal freedom, Mr. Sao had said. Perhaps he was right. What they want first of all is enough to eat . . .

CHAPTER XII

"Comrades, This Is Your Train..."

THE NEWSPAPERS!!! it suddenly says in the middle of a page of my notebook. Now what made me write that, and why all the exclamations? Oh yes, now I remember—it was on a journey to south China. We were going north again and were on our way to the railroad station, when Chi-yun suddenly stopped and grabbed my arm.

"Look at that, Karl!"

She pointed to a stack of newspapers on the platform. Next to it was a wooden box containing small coins. I could not read the Chinese characters on the box, but Chi-yun translated them for me. *Take a paper and leave five cents,* it said.

We both laughed. Imagine if that had been in the old days! The money would have been stolen as quickly as one could put it in the box, I said, but my wife shook her head. No, she said—"There wouldn't have been a cent to steal, for people would just have taken the papers."

Now the porter came with our luggage. We had better hurry up, he said; the train was leaving in a few minutes. I quickened my steps, but only as a friendly gesture. Trains never left on time in China—I knew that from bitter experience.

When he had handed me the luggage through the compartment window I asked how much I owed him. I was prepared for a violent argument—whenever one paid a porter or a rickshawman one would be accused of breaking his ricebowl and starving his children. The accusations were usually shouted at the top of the voice—the customer did not like losing face and often let himself be overcharged to avoid it.

"That will be fourteen cents," the porter answered with a

Street library – all books expressing the "incorrect" attitude have been confiscated.

In spite of all upheavals there is something unchangeable about China.

smile. That was less than fivepence—I had expected him to demand ten times as much. He now took out a ticket and wrote something on it. " Here is your receipt . . ."

He was interrupted by a stirring march from the loudspeaker in the centre of the coach. At the same movement the train began moving. I was still standing with the slip of paper in my hand; in my amazement I hardly even noticed that we left on the dot. In the China I knew, nobody had used receipts. One never used to ask people to make exact accounts—it was taken for granted that the cook and the boy and nearly everybody else kept a percentage of every sum that passed through their hands. It was not considered cheating; it was a custom . . .

" Comrades, this is your train," came a female voice over the loudspeaker. " It is your duty to keep it as clean and neat as possible. When the children want to relieve themselves, do not hold them out of the window or use the spittoon. There is a toilet at either end of the corridor . . ."

The train wound its way between softly rolling hills. The ricefields looked like giant steps, narrow at the top but broader and broader towards the foot of the hill. The farmers were gathering the harvest. They worked in large groups, men and women together. When the train roared by they stopped for a moment and looked at us from under their wide-brimmed straw hats that threw round shadows on the ground.

The villages with their graceful slanting roofs usually lay around a pond or near a brook and were shaded by tall, green bamboos. Close by was an area covered by small, regular mounds. The ancestral graves occupy about two per cent of China's arable land, or an area about half the size of England.

A man walked across a bridge. He seemed to glide under the bamboo yoke which bobbed gently up and down. Of course I could not hear it, but I felt sure that he was chanting : *eh-ho, eh-ho*! The southern Chinese usually do when they are carrying a burden.

We were alone in our compartment, but at one of the first stations we were joined by a young officer with a red star in his cap. He was accompanied by his wife and four children. Where were they from? Chi-yun guessed at central China, and

H

she turned out to be right. You could tell it from their accent. Each province has its own diaect, but the people from most of the provinces understand each other with no more difficulty than for example an Englishman and a Scotsman. Apart from the slight difference in the tones, there are certain local expressions which one has to learn when coming to a new place.

But the languages which are spoken in two of China's provinces are practically unintelligible to the rest of the people. These two provinces lie along the coast in the southern part of the country. Formerly, the people from here had to use pencil and paper when travelling in other parts of China—if they knew how to write. Once I even heard two Chinese conversing in pidgin, a primitive mixture of English and Portuguese directly translated from Chinese. Pidgin originated in the coastal towns and was used as a medium of conversation between foreigners and Chinese.

The officer told us that today practically all Chinese speak a little " national language," as the Peking dialect is called. This is something like the King's English. All Chinese schools now teach in the national language. Many Chinese learn it at the same time as they learn to read and write. The Communists are making a great effort to get rid of illiteracy. They figure that it will take them between thirty and fifty years.

By then they will try to replace the Chinese characters with a Roman alphabet. This will be a serious step, as the written language has been the main basis for national unity during China's long history. The same written language is used throughout the country. One can almost say that it has been the foundation stone of Chinese culture which began long before the building of the Pyramids and is still living.

But the characters are very complicated. There are about 60,000 of them, one for each word. Even the cleverest student cannot learn them all. If only one-fifth of them are hammered into one's head, there is not much room for other knowledge.

The Communists have decided that the characters must go. They are too heavy a drawback for a modern nation, and that is what China wants to be. But the Latin alphabet will not be introduced until everybody speaks the same language. Otherwise, each province would write the words according to its own pronunciation—the unity would disappear . . .

While we were talking to the officer, Chi-yun smoked a cigarette, dropping the ash on the floor. In the old days, everybody threw things on the floor—towards the end of a journey the passengers were ankle deep in fruit peels and pumpkin seeds and shells, mixed with spit and many other things.

Soon an attendant with broom and dustpan appeared. It was difficult to tell his expression, as he had a white cloth over his mouth and nose, but it seemed to me that he glanced reproachfully at my wife. He carefully swept up the ashes and returned a moment later to mop the floor. He also dusted a couple of times during the afternoon, and when a fly blundered into our compartment he pursued it relentlessly and then carefully removed the traces of the execution. It was the cleanest train we had ever travelled on.

In the compartment next to ours were four Europeans who turned out to be Soviet technicians. They had come to help the Chinese build up their industry. *Ding hao*—very good—was the only Chinese expression they had learned. They knew no English or German, so we could not talk to them.

The Soviet Russians in China are practically all technical advisers. There are only a few thousand of them. They receive very high pay—between two and three hundred pounds sterling a month, or about five times as much as Mao-Tse-tung gets. They are not allowed to take much money with them when they leave, so they invest their earnings in clothes, furcoats and jewellery. Some of them departed with so much luggage that people began talking about it. The Russians were then told to have no more than one suitcase each when they left the country. Soon after, a new type of giant trunk appeared on the market in Peking; each one seems large enough to contain a whole shop.

There is not much contact between the Soviet Russians and the Chinese. In Peking and Shanghai, the Russians have their own buses which other people are not allowed to use. A Chinese acquaintance told me that a couple of years ago he got to know a Soviet scientist. They liked each other, and one day my acquaintance asked the Russian to come and visit him at his home. The Russian wanted to very much, but thought it would be better to get permission first. The Chinese then wrote to the Ministry of Foreign Affairs, which replied that Chinese were advised against entertaining Soviet Russians in their homes—it was too great a responsibility in case something should happen to their guests . . .

In the dining-cars one had a choice of a dozen delicious Chinese dishes, but the Russians got potatoes and big chunks of fried meat. While the rest of us handled delicate chopsticks they worked away with knife and fork. Though they emptied one bottle of beer after the other they remained silent and morose. The beer, made in China, was just as good as Danish beer.

When the Russians got off at the first big town they were met by about a dozen Chinese. I'll never forget the change that suddenly came over the welcoming delegation. They were standing in a row on the platform, very serious and formal, almost like soldiers.

The moment they caught sight of the Russians they all smiled. " Long live the friendship between the Soviet people and the democratic people's republic of China !" they shouted. One by one they stepped forward and shook hands with the Russians who now showed that they could also smile.

The children on the train must have thought that I was a Russian. Whenever they caught sight of me they would pull their father or mother by the sleeve and say *Su lien ren*—Soviet man. Today, most of the foreigners in China are Russians.

In the old days, the children had another nickname for white men. *Yang gwei-tze,* they had called us—foreign devils —though they usually said it in a polite, even friendly way. It was quite natural for them to connect us with devils—everybody knew that the demons in the Buddhist hell had red hair like so many of the foreigners.

The children in our compartment had been quiet and obedient all day, but towards evening they became restless and cross.

" You better go over to mother and have a little self-criticism meeting," the father said, and for the next half hour the three tots sat with their mother and talked seriously. By her expressions we could tell whether she was praising or reproaching them. Then they went to sleep in one of the bunks.

That they could sleep was a wonder, for the radio was still going full blast. It was impossible to turn it off. We were entertained by endless choral singing. The melodies were Russian, the words Chinese. It was mostly something about marching forward shoulder to shoulder, sacrificing everything for the new fatherland, or the song of the democratic tractor girls. To me it all sounded like ' The Volga Boatman '.

There were also regular news broadcasts—although there was still one year to go of the first Five-Year-Plan, China had already produced her quota; production of aluminium had gone up by 2.8 per cent last month; a model worker had set a new record at the coal mines; a collective farm in the northeast reported a booming soya bean harvest.

When one was just about to fall asleep, a gong would boom, followed by loud drumbeats, the clashing of cymbals and all the accompanying sounds of a Chinese opera. Perhaps it is only to Europeans that it sounds like noise—we always search for a melody which is not there.

But next morning I came to appreciate the loudspeaker. As soon as it grew light a chorus of harking began. Everybody was brushing his teeth, scraping his tongue and clearing his throat. They spat into spittoons, decorated with Picasso's little peace dove.

Outside, the brown fields were powdered with hoar-frost. The harvest had long since been gathered; only the stubbles were left. Farmers walked next to their horse and carts which were loaded with earth or bricks. New roads cut across the flat landscape, broad dikes rose along the rivers which all ran north— uptowards the Yangtze, the great waterway of central China. In the towns, brand-new factories spewed black smoke towards the blue sky.

We shivered when we got off the train at Hankow, the main city of the Yangtze valley. For the last ten years we had spent the winters in the tropics; this was our first taste of the icy north.

Thousands of workers were building a bridge across the mighty river that divides China in two. When the bridge is completed, one will be able to go all the way from south China to the Soviet border by through-train—a journey of about five days by express train.

But now we had to cross the swift waters by ferry. When we entered the train on the opposite bank we could practically smell that we were well on our way to the north. Most southern Chinese use garlic sparingly, but the northerners eat it raw with their food. When the northerners enter a train, the flies fall down dead from the ceiling, our officer said with a smile— this is a standing joke in China.

The green bamboo groves had disappeared and the dry air chapped our lips. The wind raised clouds of dust; it somehow came in through the doors and windows and grated between our teeth. The attendant was kept busy with his mop and duster. We were approaching the great loess areas around the Yellow River.

Chinese civilization began around this river, and from here it moved south. It was mainly the river valleys that came under cultivation, and they are still the most densely populated regions in the country—580 million of China's inhabitants live in the third of the country that lies closest to the coast and in the Yangtze valley which reaches into the heart of the continent. The remaining twenty million are spread out over the enormous, barren reaches of the interior.

The voice in the loudspeaker would ocasionally tell us something about the areas which we were passing through, their main products, the number of inhabitants and what specialities one could buy at the railroad station. Chi-yun was having a wonderful time, rushing out to taste the wares at every stop. She gorged in Chinese delicacies which she had missed for years : smoked chicken, candied hawthorne berries strung on a stick, sesame seed candy. The only place where she did not buy anything was at a town where they specialized in eye medicine.

" . . . Now we are approaching Kaifeng, the cotton-production centre . . ." That was where we were getting off. Twenty

years ago, I had spent the better part of a week in Kaifeng,
searching for the last Jews of China . . .

It was a Jesuit who discovered that even China had a colony
of Jews. When he came to the Heavenly Kingdom in the early
seventeenth century, the emperor permitted him to settle down
in the capital and preach his religion. One day he received a
visit from a man who called himself *Ai*—the Chinese word for
love. The Jesuit noticed that although Ai was dressed in the
usual long robe of the Chinese, he did not have Chinese
features. His deep-set eyes were grey and he had a hooked nose.

Ai said that he came from a large town near the Yellow
River. Here lived a group of people who had a different religion
from the rest of the population, yet they were not Mohamedans. " I think we worship the same God as you," Ai said.

The Jesuit wondered whether he had stumbled upon the
descendants of a group of Nestorians who nearly a hundred
years ago had been driven out of Syria as dissenters. It was
known that they had settled down in China; the church in
Rome had occasionally heard reports about them from travel-
lers, but had not been in direct contact with them.

The two men now went into the chapel. Here the Jesuit
knelt before the Virgin and made the sign of the cross. Ai also
knelt, although reluctantly. He did not cross himself and
quickly stood up again.

" My people do not worship images," he said, " though we
do not mind kneeling before the ancestors. That is a Chinese
custom which we respect."

When he was shown a picture of the Apostles, he nodded
and said that they must be the twelve sons of Job. Virgin Mary
he mistook for Rebecca.

The Jesuit was quite disappointed when he realized that Ai
and his people were not Christians, but Jews. He spent some
hours with his visitor, however, and his notes on their conversation have added a great deal to our knowledge of the
Chinese Jews.

It is believed that the Jews came to China at the time of the
emperor Ming Ti who ruled from the year A.D. 58 to 76.
Most probably they had fled from the Romans who destroyed

Jerusalem seventy years after the birth of Christ. It must have been a fairly large migration, or else they multiplied rapidly after their arrival in China, for around the year 400 there were seventy large Jewish clans in the city of Kaifeng. They worshipped in a large synagogue built in Chinese style, but it did not face south like the Chinese temples; it was turned west—towards Jerusalem. In the most sacred room were kept thirteen holy Jewish scriptures.

Chinese history sometimes mentions officials with strange names—*Ah-tan, Ah-wu-lo-han, Ai-tze-la, Lieh-wei, Yi-tze-loh-yeh*. The Chinese could not pronounce words like Adam, Abraham, Ezra, Levi and Israel—it was the phonetic way of writing these names with Chinese characters.

Ai said that the Jews had always been well treated by the Chinese. This was probably because they did not attempt to convert others and, as far as possible, followed the customs of the country. They were not permitted to have more than one wife, however, and they kept the Sabbath holy.

The Nestorian emigrants did not fare so well in China. Welcomed at first, they were allowed to built churches in certain towns. Some of them became officials. Many of the emperors were friendly disposed towards Christianity. One of them sent out the following proclamation after having received a Catholic priest by the name of O Lo-ben (Ruben):

" The Way has more than one name, there is more than one sage. Doctrines vary in different lands, their benefits reach all mankind. O Lo-ben, a man of great virtue from Ta Tsin (The Roman Empire), has brought his images and books from afar to present them in our capital. After examining his doctrines, we find them profound and pacific. His principles . . . stress what is good and important. His teaching is not diffuse and his reasoning is sound. This religion does good to all men . . . Let it be preached freely in our empire . . . "

The Nestorians soon became famous in China for their bravery in battle. Many were given high posts in the Imperial Army. They had great influence—so great that perhaps the emperors began to fear them. Their fate is unknown, but a traveller who came to China several hundred years later re-

ported that the Nestorians and their churches had disappeared
without a trace. He had heard that there were people in China
who made the sign of the cross on solemn occasions, but it was
said that they did not even know why.

The Jesuits who came to China in the seventeenth century
did not stay very long, either. At first they converted many,
but the Pope became worried when he heard that the priests
in distant China were becoming more and more like the
Chinese. They set off fireworks during religious processions—
this was an old Chinese custom—and they permitted Chinese
converts to kowtow before the alter of their ancestors. This
was heathenish, said the Pope and forbade it. The Chinese
emperor was so offended by this that he deported the priests.

After Ai's visit to Peking we do not hear anything about
the Chinese Jews until about two hundred and fifty years later,
when a protestant missionary passed through Kaifeng. He
reported that there were only about twenty Jewish families
left in the city. The hooked noses had almost disappeared as
the result of intermarriage. The synagogue was in decay and
no one could read the Hebrew writing on the sacred parch-
ments.

When I came to Kaifeng in 1937, nothing was left of the
synagogue. I was told that the stones from the building had
been sold to the local Mohamedans who had used them for
building a mosque. I succeeded in finding one of the descendants of the Jews, an old woman whose name was Ai. I don't
usually suffer from lack of imagination, but it was impossible
even for me to see anything Jewish about her. She knew that
her ancestors were foreigners. " But I am the last one," she
said. " We have become Chinese."

But the Jews have left one trace behind in China—a
proverb. " He is stingy," one occasionally hears the Chinese
say, " he must be from Kaifeng . . ."

The locomotive whistled, and a moment later the train
pulled to a stop. We were in Kaifeng.

CHAPTER XIII

The Yellow River

AT DAYBREAK THE workers set out from their barracks. They walked in a long row, silently, each man with a shovel on his shoulder. In front of the administration building they stopped to look at the thermometer. Fourteen degrees centigrade below zero! They shivered and went on towards the river.

"The other day it was twenty degrees below," said the engineer as we got into the car. "We told the workers that they could take the day off, they would get paid anyway, but they didn't want to. They know how much is at stake. Most of them are farmers from the area that was flooded last summer."

"Don't you use forced labour also?" I asked. Despite my thick gloves, my fingers were icy.

"No, not here. We keep them away from important projects where we use machines or dynamite. Some of them still have an unfriendly attitude, so we can't trust them. They are building dikes further down the river."

He pushed the self-starter. After an unwilling cough the engine began to hum. We rolled down the road in a cloud of dust. Several times we had to use the horn. The workers had pulled down the flaps of their hats, so they could not hear us coming.

"At the moment we have only twenty thousand workers," the engineer continued. "That is enough as long as we are only doing the preparatory work. In a year or so, when we start building the dam, we will have twice as many."

The engine began to stutter. He changed into second gear, then first, but even so we had trouble making the steep hill.

It was a Czechoslovakian car of the type you see everywhere in China today. Most Chinese drivers agree that these cars have too weak engines, but the Communists praise them because they have been produced in a Peoples' Democracy. This has not prevented them from ordering eight hundred Mercedes from the capitalistic West Germans, however. These beautiful news cars, which arrived a few months ago, are reserved for officials. They always ride behind closed curtains —a custom which they have learned from their Soviet colleagues.

When we reached the top of the hill an invisible hand seemed to grab hold of the car and shake it. Up here the wind had free play. Dust came whirling like dancing dervishes. Chi-yun clutched my arm and I braced my feet against the floor, for we were driving along the edge of a ravine. The engineer nodded towards the water that was roaring deep down below.

" That is the Yellow River." He had to use the brake, for now we were going down a steep hill. " It is only a shadow of itself, but you should see it in a few months, when the snow melts in the highlands. Then it reaches all the way up there."

He pointed at the naked slope on the opposite bank. High above the yellow water was a faint line.

" I have seen the river rise sixty feet within a few hours. Then it sounds like thunder, you can barely hear yourself talk."

We came down to a suspension bridge that was nearly a hundred yards above the water. Here we got out and continued on foot. I did not dare to look right or left as we crossed the bridge. It seemed to me that it was swaying back and forth in the wind, but perhaps that was only my imagination. From a tower-like scaffold, the bridge reached out to a gigantic rock in the middle of the river and then across to the opposite bank. Chi-yun and I ran the last few yards, and we drew a sigh of relief when we again had firm ground under us.

The path on which we stood had been worn into the rock by coolies pulling boats up the river. This was the Gorge of Hell—nowhere else along the three thousand-mile course of the river is the current so strong. It took the men several days to pull a boat through the gorge.

"Do you know why the Tang Dynasty fell?" The engineer looked questioningly at me. I turned to Chi-yun. She is not only my walking dictionary, she is also my Chinese encyclopaedia. The Tang Emperors ruled from the seventh to the tenth century, she said from behind her thick scarf. Under them, the culture of China reached its greatest heights. Finally the dynasty became so weakened by a rebellion that it fell . . .

"Yes, but the river was the real bane of the Tang Dynasty," the engineer said. "It was the cause of the dissatisfaction that made the rebellion possible." He explained that at that time the emperors had their seat in a town that lay upriver, west of the gorge. The farmers paid taxes in rice. There were no roads, so the rice had to be transported upriver by boat. Every year thousands of boats were lost in the whirlpools—the strength of the nation was sapped in the Gorge of Hell. The succeeding dynasty wisely moved its capital to a town west of the gorge.

A roar interrupted him. The earth shook, and a couple of hundred yards away there was a tremendous landslide. When the dust from the explosion had settled, the workers swarmed back to work. Their swinging hammers crushed the rocks into pieces that were shovelled into baskets and carried down to the place where the first section of the dam was to be built. Steel struck sparks against stones; the carriers moved in endless, untiring rows. Thus you move mountains in China.

The Yellow River waters about forty per cent of China's agricultural land. For three thousand years the Chinese have kept a record of the river, and during this period it has overflowed one thousand five hundred times. It is estimated that several hundred million people have drowned in its waters or starved to death during ensuing famines. There are no exact figures for this, but it is known that during the last big flood— that was in 1938 when Chiang Kai-shek's troops dynamited the dikes in order to stop the advancing Japanese—eight hundred and eighty thousand people were drowned.

Once the river had its outlet near Peking. Later it changed its course and flowed close to Shanghai, nearly one thousand miles to the south. Then it changed back to its present bed south of Peking.

No other river in the world is so muddy, the engineer told us, not even the Nile. If one takes a yearly average, it carries only one point seven pounds of mud per cubic yard of water. The Yellow River carries fifty seven pounds per cubic yard, and when it rises after a big rain it can reach as much as nine hundred and seventy-five pounds!

" If you took all the mud which the river washes into the Yellow Sea during a year and used it for building a wall one yard wide and one yard high, it would encircle the world twenty-three times at the Equator," the engineer told us.

Most of the mud comes from the fertiles loess areas of north-west China. This is hilly terrain, and at some places the rain-water washes away as much as half an inch of soil every year.

How can man put a stop to the floods and this terrible erosion. From the time of the first emperors, the rulers of China have pondered over this problem. For three thousand years it was the practice to build dikes, but they had to be made higher and higher, for the river kept raising itself by its own deposits, and sooner or later it would break through.

In 1946, Chiang Kai-shek flew a group of American engineers to the Yellow River. After a short survey, they declared that the only solution was to build a series of dams and simultaneously plant large belts of forest. This would take around a century, they said, and require more machinery than China could ever pay for ...

The engineer smiled. " In new China we do not measure such things in dollars and cents. Perhaps that is why we have not let ourselves be discouraged by the difficulties. We are going to build forty-four dams altogether. The largest and by far the most important one will be here at the Gorge of Hell. This dam alone will be able to prevent floods. It will be completed in 1962."

A man with a red flag came towards us. In a little while there would be another explosion. We went under a ledge where some workers had already gathered. They nodded and made room for us.

" Most of these workers will soon be homeless," the engineer continued. " The wall of the dam will span the river just about where the hanging bridge is now." He made a sweeping gesture which took in most of the river valley. "All this will be under water. There will be a lake of more than five hundred square miles, so we will have to evacuate more than half a million people."

The artificial lake will easily be able to absorb the water even after a heavy rain, so the danger of flood will disappear. The mud will settle at the bottom of the lake, so the water will eventually run clear—"maybe we will have to change the name of the river," he added with a grin.

He explained to the workers what he had just told us. They nodded. Yes, the new dam would prevent floods. They would lose their homes, but the government had promised them new and better ones elsewhere. And all the people living near the river would be better off, all China would be better off when the dam was finished. This they had learned at the political meetings in the evenings . . .

"The dam here at the Gate of Hell will be the second largest in the world," the engineer went on. "It will have a drop of about two hundred feet. We have already ordered the turbines from the Soviet Union. They will produce four thousand six hundred million kilowatt-hours a year—more than enough to supply three provinces with electricity even after the towns become industrialized."

He looked out over the barren winter landscape and smiled. In his mind the hills were already covered with forest, water from the artificial lake irrigated fertile fields, humming turbines powered new industrial plants.

"But there are many difficulties ahead," he continued soberly—one of the latest political campaigns emphasized that a good Marxist should never underestimate his problems, he should be humble and criticize himself. "We figure that it will take around fifty years to complete the project. It will be considerably larger than the T.V.A. project in the United States. The beginning is especially difficult because we have so little machinery, almost everything has to be done by hand, but once we begin to produce our own machinery we will be able to speed up . . ."

The dams will form a gigantic staircase along the middle section of the river. Fields which now lack water during the dry season will be irrigated all year round once the artificial lakes are completed. Instead of bringing misery to the people, the river will give them riches—it will produce ten times as much electricity as the whole nation now consumes . . .

Again his eyes became dreamy. I could understand his enthusiasm. Never before had China attempted to carry out so great a project . . .

Again there was a roar. Chi-yun and I squeezed ourselves up against the rocks. The workers laughed, and even before the stones had stopped raining down from the sky they were hurrying back to the job.

CHAPTER XIV

The City God

WE WOKE EARLY on our first morning in Shanghai. The waiters at the hotel had not appeared yet; for half an hour we had to wait for breakfast. As soon as we had finished eating we went out in the city.

First we went to The Bund. This used to be the heart of Shanghai: a segment of Manhattan, transplanted to the banks of a muddy Chinese river. Here lie the great business houses from where a handful of whites for nearly a century controlled the foreign trade of China.

When we came to the former Hong Kong and Shanghai Bank we both stopped. Yes, they were still there—the two venerable British bronze lions which for so many years have guarded the entrance. An acquaintance had told us that they were removed some time after the Communists took over. For more than a year they were absent—this was during the purges—but one day suddenly they were there again.

" Now they are harmless," the Chinese said jokingly. " They have also had their brains washed."

Many other stories are told about the first days of the Communists in Shanghai. They came here straight from the country; most of the troops were peasants who had never seen a big city before. A soldier let out a roar and charged a mirror with fixed bayonet—he took his own reflection for an enemy. Another soldier tried to blow out an electric bulb when he wanted to sleep. Some made fires under the bathtubs in the apartments where they had been billeted. How else could one get a hot bath?

In the Shanghai I knew, traffic had always been hectic on

First and foremost it is the young that the communists try to win over.

Sugar-coated hawthorn berries on a stick is a Chinese delicacy.

The Bund at this time of the morning. Pedestrians hurried along the sidewalks; the Chinese are usually a calm people, but the atmosphere of the big town had infected them. A chorus of angry horns would sound whenever a rickshaw coolie got in the way of the endless rows of motor cars.

Now a lonely bus came rumbling by. An old woman crossed the street without looking right or left. She walked up to one of the lions and stroked its paw. It was worn shiny by all the hands that had touched it in passing, taking along a little of the lion's strength.

We both looked at a building lying close by. Then we smiled and took each other by the hand. Up there on the fifth floor, in the Danish Consulate, we had become man and wife seventeen years ago.

"Do you remember the consul?" Chi-yun asked as we walked on. I certainly did! He first refused to marry us; in his opinion it was a step down for a white to marry a Chinese . . .

"Didn't he thaw up and give you a bouquet of flowers at the ceremony? As far as I remember . . ."

I broke off in the middle of the sentence. We had come to the Shanghai Club, and suddenly I remembered an episode which I had not thought of for years. Now I related it to Chi-yun.

One day—it must be more than twenty years ago—I was arguing with a rickshawman here in front of the club. He had pulled me a long way and said that twenty cents was too little. He was probably right, but that was all I had on me.

A crowd quickly gathered. They sided with the coolie, but the quarrel was interrupted by a bearded Sikh from Shanghai's international police. The Sikh did not even bother to find out who was right. You better stop making a fuss here, he said to the coolie, or I will take away your cushion. That was the usual punishment for rickshawmen; they had to pay a dollar to get the cushion back at the police station.

The coolie immediately gave up. I can still see him as he walked away with his rickshaw, his skinny back glistening with perspiration. I thanked the Sikh and went up the stairs . . .

I

Now I was ashamed—just the thought makes my cheeks burn—but at the time it had seemed quite natural to me. I was white and Shanghai was the white man's city.

The old signboard had disappeared from the entrance. " Shanghai Club, members only ", it had said. Now some Chinese characters announced that it was a democratic sailors' palace.

It would be fun to see the place again, I thought, but when I went up the stairs a doorman came out and stopped me. Was I a sailor? I showed him my press card, but he just glanced at it and shook his head.

Chi-yun laughed. " Before, only whites could enter here," she said. " Now it would have been better to be a Chinese. How times have changed!"

At the entrance to the next building, a Sikh was sitting on an empty wooden box. How tame he looked in his civilian clothes! When we stopped to chat with him, he told us that he had been a policeman in the old days. Just the thought of it made him straighten his back. Now he was watchman for the English firm which owned the building—a boring job. Fifty or sixty people came and left every day, that was all. Shanghai was a dead city.

He gazed at the river. There used to be dozens of big ships and hundred of junks and sampans. Now the long wharves were empty but for two small steamers.

The Sikh worked for Sassoon, formerly one of the biggest men in Shanghai. Sir Victor Sassoon, an English Jew, made a fortune in the China trade. When the Communists came to power his property in Shanghai was worth more than £5,000,000. He decided to try to make a go of it under the Reds—he might just as well, since he could not take his luxury hotels and modern apartment houses with him.

At first he managed all right. The hotels were leased to Chinese firms and there was no trouble renting out the apartments. But after a couple of years the government began to impose fines for past offences which had not been considered unlawful before. At the same time, heavy new taxes were imposed. Soon the money which Sassoon had to pay exceeded his earnings—and he had to pay on the dot. If not, he was fined an extra three per cent a day! It has since been lowered to one per cent. " We do not want to be unreasonable," the Communists declared.

Today, Sir Victor Sassoon owes the Chinese Government slightly over £1,000,000. The authorities are probably waiting for the debt to surpass the value of the property. This should not take long. Then the government will announce that it is willing to call it quits—it will lose a little on it, but as a gesture of friendship . . .

One does not have to be a crystal gazer to predict this. Practically all the foreigners who had business property in China have already been through the mill . . .

We walked on and soon came to a junk which was tied up alongside The Bund. Some children were playing hide-and-seek aboard the high, clumsy-looking vessel. The smallest ones were tethered with long pieces of rope. A woman pulled a pail of water up from the river; her black pigtail swung back and forth as she hauled at the rope. She was washing clothes with water the colour of strong tea.

In the prow sat three men smoking their pipes. They nodded when we asked if we were allowed to come on board. It was not easy to understand their Shanghai dialect, but we did find out that the junk had formerly belonged to the oldest one of them, a man by name of Wang. A year ago the boat had been taken over by the Democratic Association of River Workers. This was a kind of union; it managed the business affairs of the crew and paid them their salaries, about six pounds sterling a month for each man. The former owner received about ten per cent more than the others as a form of compensation.

" Is the arrangement better than the old one?" I asked. Wang puffed at his pipe.

" The profit is not as large as before, but then I have no more responsibilities."

One of the men said that it was advantageous to belong to the association. When your wife was to give birth to a child, she could stay at the hospital free of charge. The association had a club where you could get cheap meals. You no longer risked losing your job when times were bad.

"Your junk still has eyes," I remarked. This is an old custom—one large eye is painted on either side of the prow. A boat must also be able to see.

"Yes, but we know now that such things are superstition," Wang replied. "We have learned it at the meetings. The gods do not decide for us, we are masters of our own fate."

This is quite a change from the old days. The people who ply the river used to be especially superstitious—if someone who could not swim fell into the water, he did not have much chance. Nobody wanted to save him, for the river would revenge itself if you deprived it of its victim. Even if a reward was promised, the rescue would often be postponed until one could be sure that the unfortunate man had already drowned. From a Chinese point of view this was very sensible. The river god got his victim, the relatives of the deceased escaped the wrath of the forefathers, for they had the body, and the rescuer earned his reward . . .

The children waved goodbye to us. We no longer walked in the shadow of the skyscrapers, for here the houses were low and had Chinese roofs. We had reached the outskirts of Nantao, Shanghai's old Chinatown.

"I wonder what they are waiting for," I said to Chi-yun, pointing at a queue several hundred feet long. Many of the people stared at us as we walked by. Perhaps it was because we were still holding hands; one seldom sees that in China.

At the head of the queue we found out that they were buying toilet paper—six large sheets was all that each person was allowed, as there was a shortage at the moment. In Red China, many people automatically join a queue when they see one, and only then do they ask what is on sale. It is almost bound to be something they need, for there are always shortages—most of all of food. It is not unusual for housewives to get up at three or four o'clock in the morning and join a queue; if she comes later, the things she needs may be sold out.

Pregnant women are given special consideration; they don't have to stand in line with the rest, but are served right away.

Often, however, there are so many of them that they form a queue of their own.

Not long ago the newspapers told of a woman who stood in the queue for those who were pregnant. Suddenly her tummy fell down on the ground—it was a pillow. The newspapers said that this was a most unpatriotic act . . .

" Hello, master ! "

A pedlar of oranges had spoken to me in English. Oranges are cheap in China, and very juicy. One can get them practically all year round. They come down the Yangtze by boat from Szechuan, the great, fertile province in the south-western part of the country.

The orange-seller told me that he had once served as a boy in a foreign family. He was sorry that the foreigners had left; things had been better when they were here—selling oranges was not nearly as profitable as his old job. There was also too much politics these days, he thought.

" All the time go meeting, talkie, talkie Mao Tse-tung," was how he expressed it in his pidgin-English.

In Peking, nobody would have dared to make such a remark. The northerners have always been the most compliant of the Chinese. They have learned to swim with the current—time and again, they have bowed silently before foreign rulers. Practically all the rebellions in the history of China were started by southerners. The great majority of the high Communist leaders are also from south China.

In the capital, we had never heard as much as a rumour about organized resistance to the government. But shortly before we came to Shanghai, one of the local· papers had admitted that there was growing resistance against the authorities in the former international city. *Hsin Wen Jih Pao,* was the name of this paper, and it wrote on November 30, 1956 : " In the recent one or two months, secret agents and sabotage activities have been on the increase in schools, factories, streets and lanes. Reactionary letters of intimidation as well as mimeographed pamphlets have been circulated, expressing dissatisfaction with wages, welfare and supply conditions. Serious crimes for political and personal vengeance motives, as well as thefts and larceny proceeding from corruption of morals and dissipation, have also increased steadily. The public security bureau urges its members to be vigilant ..."

When the Communists first took over power, the Shanghai Chinese stopped speaking English. If Europeans asked a shop attendant something in English, he would pretend not to understand. People knew that the new rulers were prejudiced against the western nations as well as their languages. That was when everyone was beginning to study Russian.

Some months ago, the government began its new, "liberal" course. Now the Chinese no longer had to consider the capitalist nations as enemies—Mao Tse-tung even encouraged the students to study English.

The day after his speech, smiling shop attendants in Shanghai again addressed their European customers in English ...

When Chi-yun and I entered the narrow lanes of Nantao, we soon realized that Europeans had become an unusual sight here. In the old days, the "Chinatown" was visited by so many Europeans that the people hardly noticed them. There were then around one hundred thousand whites in Shanghai. Today there are around five hundred.

Many of the children in Nantao had probably never seen a white man before. They crowded around me, pointing and shouting—look, a foreigner! It was impossible to break through this living wall of people; not until a policeman came were we able to move on.

"He must be a Soviet-man," I heard someone say.

"No," came the reply, "his clothes are different from theirs—he has narrow pants and he is smartly dressed."

I looked triumphantly at my wife, but unfortunately she had not heard it. She always complains that I dress like a vagabond. All the Soviet men have bell-bottom trousers; it must be a Russian fashion.

The Soviet Russians are not as highly thought of in Shanghai as elsewhere in China. A couple of years ago, the Russians held grand exhibitions in all the large Chinese cities. In Peking the exhibits were admired, but a Chinese friend told me that one often heard critical remarks at the Shanghai exhibition. "That's nothing to show people," the blasé Shanghailanders said. "We had much finer goods in our own stores before liberation."

Curious faces were watching me from doors and windows. What a lot of people there were; The Communists have tried to reduce the population in Shanghai, for strategic reasons. Early in 1955, the city had a population of 6,100,000. During that year, 800,000 Shanghailanders were sent to the interior. But when another census was taken at the end of the year, it turned out that the city now had a population of 6,300,000!

Where had they all come from? Nobody knows exactly. My friends thought that the majority of the new arrivals were farmers who were dissatisfied with the poor living conditions in the country...

From some of the windows came the familiar rattle of mahjongg bricks. This game was at first prohibited by the Communists; it belonged to the sinful past. Last year it was permitted again, but people are not supposed to play for money.

Spearheaded by the policeman, we made our way to the Nantao temple. In Peking, most temples have been converted into schools; the rest are empty. People are careful—if you burn incense to the gods, you risk being considered superstitious and reactionary. But Nantao's old temple was humming with activity—people even had to queue up and await their turns to kowtow before the dusty idols. Even the large, dark hall on the first floor, where people seldom came in the old days, was crowded. Incense and smoke from the many little fires of paper money made the eyes smart.

An attendant told us that the temple had formerly been administered by a religious guild. Now it was managed by a committee elected by the people. Each attendant was in charge of one or several gods. They had to keep the place clean; in return, they got a percentage of the income from the sale of incense and paper money.

During the first few years after the liberation, the temple had operated at a loss. "I did not get very much rice," the plump, friendly attendant told us. Only old people came—perhaps they were less afraid of the Communists than of the consequences of not sacrificing to the gods.

About a year ago, it somehow became known that it was all right to go to the temple again. People came streaming—on certain festivals, the crowds were bigger than they had ever been before the liberation.

" Which is the most popular god?" I asked.

" The city god of Shanghai," the attendant replied with a smile, and added, " Fortunately." This god was his " concession ". He added that the god of wealth was also very popular.

" Plenty good luck again!" he said, rubbing his hands. Just then a gong boomed. He nodded to us and went over to his god to burn a fresh stick of incense.

CHAPTER XV

Teacher Of Virtue

MAO TSE-TUNG looked down fatherly at us from his traditional place of honour on the wall facing the door. Otherwise there wasn't a soul in the studio meeting-room where the interview was to take place. I sat down in one of the easy chairs. My heart was hammering, for we had run to avoid being late.

"I told you so," I said to Chi-yun. "There was no need to hurry—film stars are never on time. I know them. We'll probably have to wait for hours..."

Just then there were footsteps outside. I jumped up and straightened my tie, but at the sight of the girl who entered I sat down again, a little sheepishly. We were waiting for Miss Shih Wei, I said.

"I am Miss Shih Wei."

Chi-yun told me afterwards that the disappointment was written all over my face. You could hardly blame me for that. Here I was expecting a Chinese Marilyn Monroe, but the girl in the flat shoes looked more like a schoolteacher without her glasses. Even powder and lipstick could hardly have made her pale face glamorous, and if she had any exciting curves they were well hidden beneath her loose blue trousers and jacket.

What on earth can one write about her, I thought: she seems completely colourless. I doubt whether she would have minded much even if I had said it aloud. We had not talked with her for more than a few minutes before she said that an actor should not have too strong a personality.

"It is easier for the masses to identify themselves with a plain, ordinary type. The actor as a person should not attract too much attention. Individual performances must not over-shadow the message of the film . . ."

She sat with her hands folded in her lap, very serious. Her name could hardly suit her better, I thought. Shih Wei means *Teacher of Virtue*.

What kind of message should a film have? She replied that it should first of all strengthen the class-consciousness of the people. " The audience must be able to distinguish clearly between its friends and its enemies. A film should also strengthen the masses in their belief in the new society—other· wise it has no justification."

Miss Shih Wei told us that twice a week she and her colleagues attended political meetings. " It is here we get our inspiration. We discuss the government's plans and try to co-ordinate our work with them. One must always maintain close contact with the problems of the nation."

When a Chinese script writer today gets an idea for a film, he first discusses it with the actors. If they think that it sounds promising from an ideological as well as a political point of view, they go out among the people and live in the milieu which the film is to depict. They try to find the right " types " and study them at close hand. Miss Shih Wei had once spent six weeks in a coalmining town in North China. She had also lived among farmers and factory workers.

" From the people, to the people," she quoted from Mao Tse-tung, looking reverently up at his picture.

I had heard that she had played a street girl in one of her latest films. She nodded.

" But how could you find a model? After all, there are no longer street girls in China."

" No, that was quite a problem, but then I got hold of a comic-strip from before the liberation. There I found the right type."

The Chinese Communists have often said that one of their aims is to get rid of all class distinction. Everybody must learn to feel and think like workers. Miss Shih Wei was a living proof that they have succeeded in some cases. " My work," she said, where European actors would have talked about their art.

Every morning she came to the studio at eight o'clock and stayed until four, with an hour off for lunch.

" But what if they are shooting a film—don't you stay longer then ?"

" No, we never work overtime."

Despite the " Miss ", she was married and had three children. Two of them she saw only during weekends; they were at a government nursery. The third one was only a year old and lived with her and her husband, who was a government official. " My beloved," she called him. This expression has been introduced by the Communists who consider it more " progressive " than the old-fashioned way of addressing one's spouse. Not many Chinese women can say " my beloved " without wincing, however.

We learned that Chinese film actors are divided into sixteen different categories whose salaries range from nine pounds sterling to forty-five pounds a month. Miss Shih Wei was in the tenth category and earned slightly more than ten pounds.

" Can one say that this is a measure of an actor's popularity ?"

" No, it depends just as much on seniority and effort. We try to avoid building up stars. We do not want a few to get all the attention—that is undemocratic . . ."

The Communists have also tried to distribute the star-lustre more evenly within the theatre. They made a point of replacing a popular actor with his understudy without notice. The people must learn to appreciate the idea behind a play rather than an individual performance, they said.

But the public rebelled. When the understudy entered the stage the audience would boo and whistle and demand its money back. It did not help that the press started a campaign against such outbursts of " obstinate and undemocratic individualism ". The authorities finally had to discontinue the practice.

Miss Shih Wei, who was twenty-eight, had only been working in films for a few years. Before that she had performed in Chinese operas. This had been very tiring work, she said, as

the performances usually began at four in the afternoon and
continued until midnight . . .

Europeans find it hard to understand why the majority of
Chinese prefer opera to the cinema. I recently met a Danish
salesman who was on a business trip to China. Some Chinese
acquaintances had invited him to the opera.

" There was no scenery or anything," he told me. " The
actors ran around on the stage, screaming and yelling, and
the orchestra sounded like boys banging away on tin cans. I
didn't want to be impolite to my hosts, but after an hour or
so I just couldn't stand it any more, my ears ached."

No wonder the performances are so noisy. There are really
not supposed to be walls or a ceiling to hurl the sound back
at you. When the first operas were shown—that was under the
Mongols in the thirteenth century—there were no theatres in
China. The performances took place in the open air, so the
actors had to shout to make themselves heard, and the
musicians had to bang away at their instruments. They still do.

When an actor first enters the stage he announces his name
and role. This is really unnecessary, for the audience already
knows all about him from his dress and make-up. If he carries
a fan he is a scholar. A peasant feather in the hat signifies
a general. Those dressed entirely in black are invisible. Crafty
officials have their faces painted white. Generals have red faces
—a custom from the Sung dynasty, when military leaders
used make-up to hide their unwarlike paleness.

I vividly remember the first Chinese opera I attended. Chi-
yun was with me. She had promised to explain the plot to
me, but even so I could not understand much of it.

" Why is that fellow waving a whip?" I asked.

" Because he is on horseback."

" Why does the general suddenly step on a chair?"

" He is mounting the city wall . . ."

A while later the actors sat down on the floor and began
making funny movements with their arms. What on earth was
the idea of that?

" Have you no imagination?" Chi-yun asked. " Anybody
can see that they are rowing."

One of the rowers began waving a black flag with white stripes. The waves became higher, they were drowning—everybody knew this except me, and I no longer felt like asking, I did not want to be accused of being unimaginative . . .

Thanks to the opera, even the poorest Chinese farmer knows the more dramatic episodes from his country's long history. During our conversation with Miss Shih Wei I asked whether all the popular old operas were still being performed. No, she said. After the Communists came to power, the opera companies had been given a list of the plays that were " desirable ".

" Of course we do not want to perform plays which are in the old, feudalistic spirit," she explained. " If you make a virtue of servility and submissiveness, the people will learn to think incorrectly."

Miss Shih Wei said that even some of the " approved " plays had been altered a little—the bad characters had been made worse, the good ones better. Otherwise the audience might easily be bewildered. The message of the play should be as clear and simple as possible.

" We have reformed and developed the various national arts," she said. " But this national inheritance can only serve the people after it has been re-evaluated from our new ideological point of view."

Much of China's literature has also been discarded or " simplified ". When the Communists took over, one of the largest publishing houses in the country had eight thousand eight hundred titles in stock. When the directors of the company had been " re-educated ", they were told to compile a list of those books which were suitable for new China. Of course they wanted to play safe, so the list which they finally handed in contained only one thousand two hundred titles. The rest of the books went back to the papermill.

A Yugoslav journalist whom I know recently interviewed Lao Sheh, the author of *Rickshaw Boy*. The journalist told Lao Sheh that he would like to translate this book into his own language.

" Better wait a few months," the famous old author said. " Then there will be a new edition of the book in Russian."

He explained that the old central figure had not been sufficiently " positive " in his attitude—he had laughed at his troubles and not taken up the struggle. Lao Sheh had therefore changed him a little, and it would be better for the Yugoslavs to be introduced to the new, class-conscious *Rickshaw Boy*...

Miss Shih Wei thought that it was perfectly justified to make such alterations. In her opinion, the main purpose of art was to serve the State. Other Chinese Communists share her opinion, or at least they say so—all except one.

That one is Hu Feng. When you mention his name in China, people become silent or quickly change the subject. Once I asked an official from the Foreign Office to tell me something about Hu Feng. He was usually very helpful, but on this occasion he stiffened. " No comment," he said.

Hu Feng is a writer and literary critic who made a name for himself after the liberation. Everybody considered him a good Communist, but about two years ago he wrote an essay on a classical Chinese novel called *The Dream of the Red Chamber,* hinting that they could be other views on art than the strictly Marxist one.

The article caused a stir in literary circles throughout the country. Nobody had dared to say such a thing before. The authorities ordered Hu Feng to write a denunciation of his own views, and so he did—but most of his self-criticism turned out to be a subtle defence of liberalism and individual freedom.

Only after this " self-criticism " had been published did the Communists discover that they had walked into a trap. Now the Chinese have always had a special ability to hide their innermost feelings, to nod and smile when the situation demands. Perhaps it is this knowledge which makes the Communists so sensitive about traitors within their own ranks. Hu Feng was arrested and a nation-wide campaign started against him. The authorities insisted that there was a Hu Feng conspiracy among the intellectuals. Thousands were arrested.

When Hu Feng's earlier writings were examined, they turned out to be studded with ambiguous statements. The life-histories and confessions of a large number of people were examined for signs of similar "hidden obstructionism". Newspapers and books published since the liberation were also gone through by patriotic committees—a kind of Chinese "Un-American Activities Committees".

Many public institutions were closed for weeks while the investigations were going on. At Yenching, my old university, they also seached for "traitors". All they found was an anti-Communist slogan on a wall in one of the toilets.

One student was accused of being a secret admirer of Hu Feng and of having exchanged letters with like-minded people. When he denied this, his progressive schoolmates decided to lock him up in his room until he confessed. Three-quarters of a year passed before he broke down.

The authorities called Hu Feng all the usual names reserved for enemies of Communism. Even so, many came to realize what he stood for. He was against blind imitation of the Soviet Union. He desired an independent Chinese Communism and greater academic freedom.

The authorities must finally have realized that the attacks on Hu Feng had the opposite of the desired effect. I have been told that many people who had never felt the lack of freedom began to wonder. There might be something to what Hu Feng had said, since everyone was so excited about it—perhaps it would be better with a little freedom ...

The campaign against Hu Feng was dropped as suddenly as it had started. Some months later the government introduced many of the reforms which he had indirectly advocated. Scientists were permitted to criticize Soviet methods and theories, professors were exempted from attending so many meetings, students were encouraged to study other languages than Russian, and a campaign was started to make people express themselves without fear.

"Let a hundred flowers bloom, let a hundred different familes speak their minds", was the name of this campaign which was in full swing when Chi-yun and I arrived in China. Every time we said to a Communist that there was a lack of freedom, he would cite the flower-slogan.

One day we talked to a high official from the Ministry of

Education. It was a good thing, I said, that the government had started this campaign—it proved that they wanted to give the intellectuals more freedom of expression.

" Well, it actually isn't so much to please the intellectuals," he replied. " We realized that we were beginning to stagnate in the field of science for want of fresh ideas. The real purpose of the campaign is to achieve better scientific ideas."

Was it Hu Feng who caused a change-over to a more liberal course in China? Or was it Stalin's death? Probably a combination of both. Hu Feng is still locked up, but he is expected to be released soon. It is whispered that the Communists now recognize his talent and that he will be offered a high post when the episode is no longer so fresh in the minds of the people . . .

I did not mention Hu Feng during my conversation with Miss Shih Wei. Why should I embarrass her? The government no longer attacked him, but neither had he been restored to favour, so people hardly knew what to think.

She told me that being a foreigner, it would be hard for me to understand the change in the Chinese people since the liberation. Their way of looking at life was different—one could also tell this by their taste in movies.

" We Chinese do not care much for pure entertainment any more," she said. " The foreign films which were so popular before the liberation would not be appreciated any more. They belong to the past—now the people demand a more positive line . . ."

On our way home we passed a cinema. Outside was the longest queue we had ever seen. There was an English film on the programme—the first one to be shown in China after the liberation. The ticket window would not be opened for several hours, but the people did not seem to mind waiting.

white man?
ou don't see
any in new
hina.

hi-yun *(second
om right)*
ith her
other, sister
nd
rother-in-law.

In Peking—today Chinese cities are full places like this where you can read the newspapers.

A cobbler at work in Peking.

eryone wants
dress like a
nple factory
orker and you
ldom see
yone wearing
ake-up—not
en this
anghai
m-star.

ehind the
enes at the
pera these two
omen are
essed as high
ficials.

Everyone wear the padded cotton suits, usually blue for the grown-ups and red for the children.

A wandering tinsmith at work in North China.

CHAPTER XVI

Mr. Lin Eats Pepper

IT WAS EVENING. Mr. Lin, who wore European clothes, had pulled his chair away from the lamp. One could not see his face clearly, but his balding head glowed in the semi-darkness. As he talked, he toyed with his watchchain. He had small, plump hands—that was considered a sign of luck in the old days, perhaps because the God of Wealth had fat hands.

It would be no exaggeration to say that Mr. Lin had been born with a silver spoon in his mouth. His father was one of the first Chinese to start a spinning mill in Shanghai. When he died, he had five large factories which he left his son.

True enough, the factories no longer belonged to Mr. Lin. They had been taken over by the state, but he had been compensated. He was still so wealthy that the press called him " the last Chinese millionaire." The Communists displayed him to visitors as a shining example of a reformed industrial tycoon.

Mr. Lin told us that he had had many vices in the old days. He kept mistresses, drank too much, ate too much, and he also gambled. There was self-reproach in his voice, yet I had a feeling that he rather enjoyed talking about his former dissipation.

Just before the Communists came to Shanghai, Mr. Lin had fled to Hong Kong with a million American dollars. " It did not even occur to me to remain in China." He had heard that the Communists executed all rich people.

Hong Kong is one of the most beautiful cities in the world, but also one of the most heartless. There are over a million refugees from the mainland. A few thousand of them are rolling in money, the rest live on the edge of starvation.

Mr. Lin did not feel at home in the small, crowded colony. He had intended to invest his money, but everything seemed so uncertain to him. The Communists could take Hong Kong any moment they felt like it.

One day he read a speech by Mao Tse-tung. "Chairman Mao asked all Chinese business people who had fled to return. New China needed our help," he said. "We would be justly treated—if we had earned our money in an honest way, we would be allowed to keep it."

Mr. Lin's friends had laughed when he told them that he was thinking of returning to Shanghai. You are crazy, they said. You can't trust the Reds. They will put you before a peoples' court and shoot you.

"Of course the possibility was there—but I was sick and tired of the empty life in Hong Kong. I was nearly sixty, I wanted to die in my own country. I also had a feeling that Chairman Mao would keep his word."

Mr. Lin had been speaking perfectly naturally, but now he straightened himself in the chair and cleared his throat. His round face turned serious. He did not look at us, it was as if he were talking to the wall.

"In the Democratic Peoples' Republic I have learned the joy of working hand-in-hand with the people. I used to be a capitalist exploiter, so of course the people had only contempt for me. Thanks to the Communists I have come to realize how deplorable my former way of life was. I was selfish and lived only for myself, therefore I was dissatisfied. Now that I have changed my attitude, the people has received me with open arms. It is a pleasure to walk among the workers and know that they consider you a friend. I am proud to take part in the reconstruction of China under the inspiring leadership of Chairman Mao and the Communist Party."

In China, the Communists received him like a prodigal son. They can be merciless towards "enemies of the people," but by coming home, Mr. Lin had proved that he had the "correct" attitude. The newspapers praised him for his patriotic act. There is more happiness in heaven over one sinner . . .

A brief investigation proved that he had not earned his money in an "immoral" way; he was known to have been against Chiang Kai-shek. He was again put in charge of his factories. " I also headed a group of progressive capitalists who were to help prepare the way for socialism in China . . ."

I was about to ask whether that was not rather like digging your own grave, but Mr. Lin went on talking. While he was away, the Communists had introduced a new economic set-up —" a transitory stage," they called it. The net income from all privately-owned enterprises in the country was to be divided into four equal parts. One went to the state, one to the workers, one was used for re-investment, and the last part went to the owner. This arrangement was to continue until China was " ready for socialism."

Mr. Lin was no longer in sole charge of his factories. He shared the responsibility with a young Communist who looked after the interests of the state and the workers. Mr. Lin told us that he had always got along very well with his Communist associate. " We solved all problems in a spirit of mutual respect and understanding."

One of my Chinese acquaintances from the old days, a businessman, had given me a slightly different description of the relationship with these " political directors " who were posted in all large firms. " They were really more like spies," he said. " When the Communists first came, they knew nothing about business. They considered it anti-social by nature, yet they realized that it was necessary and that they had to learn from us. Otherwise they could not maintain trade connections with the rest of the world, and they needed trade. To them, we capitalists were a kind of wild animals which had to be studied while they were being tamed. The political directors had access to all our books, so of course they soon learned our methods as well as our trade secrets . . ."

When Mr. Lin returned to Shanghai he knew nothing about Marxism. " It did not interest me very much, either, but I soon realized that I would have to learn something about it. Otherwise I could not hold my own in discussions with the union representatives and with my Communist colleagues. I started attending political lectures and meetings and before I knew it, I had been convinced by the striking logic and justice in the arguments which I had set out to refute ! "

Mr. Lin smiled, pleased with the fine phrase he had just completed.

About a year ago, the Communists had made a decisive step towards their final goal: state socialism. All industrial and business enterprises were taken over by the government, but the former owners remained as managers. Now they no longer got a share of the profits—they were state employees on a fixed salary. Mr. Lin's salary was seventy-five pounds a month.

He got an additional £25,000 a year from the state, or about five per cent of the value of his former factories. This payment will continue for seven years, until he has received a little over one-third of the value of his factories. All the ex-capitalists will receive such annual payments—it is a form of compensation, intended to win their good-will.

The government has been surprisingly successful in securing the co-operation of the business people. This is partly because of the rottenness of the Chiang Kai-shek government in its last days. It taxed business people so heavily that they could hardly exist. Corrupt officials sold monopolies to the highest bidders. *Anything* will be better than Chiang, people said.

The Communists are at least honest, and even those business people who dislike them cannot help admiring them. No one can deny that they are good organizers. All Chinese are proud that China can now produce many of the " strategic " goods which were put on the embargo list at the time of the Korean war.

The Chinese are among the best business people in the world. Did Mr. Lin not fear that they would lose their initiative under the new system?

When he shook his head, I told him how Chi-yun and I that same day had entered a store on one of Shanghai's main streets. Nobody came to serve us, so we went over to a clerk who was reading a newspaper. I explained that I wanted a vest.

" We don't have any."

" But I just saw one in your window."

" We don't have your size."

" I would like to try it—it looked as if it would fit me."

" It would be useless," he said and continued reading.

We had heard many Chinese complain that one did not get good service any more. In some shops, the attendants make up accounts during the middle of the month. If they have already made enough to cover expenses and salaries, they take it easy during the rest of the month. Formerly, one could get a suit made in a couple of days. Now it takes months—the tailors are also government-employees. The same is true of the artisans. A European diplomat we knew had had a leaking faucet for nearly half a year. No one had the time to come and repair it.

" On our way to China we visited Yugoslavia," I told Mr. Lin. " The Yugoslavs also introduced state socialism just after the war, but four or five years later they gave it up. Production kept going down . . ."

" Oh, but it is different in China," Mr. Lin protested. " We Chinese have become so patriotic after the liberation—we are no longer interested in personal gains . . ."

The disbelief in my face seemed to bother him. " Of course there are certain difficulties in the beginning," he quickly added. " The road to socialism is not easy, but we will overcome all obstacles. I myself asked the authorities to take over my factories—I was one of the first ones to do so. You must not forget that everything has been voluntary in China, it is the will of the people . . ."

I protested. My Chinese acquaintance had not been a bit enthusiastic about giving up his firm. " But there was no other way," he told me. " We could not get raw materials from the state—it only supplied those who were progressive. The workers were encouraged to strike against us, taxes became heavier and heavier, and we were fined for all sorts of past offences. Then when the government had brought us to the edge of bankruptcy, it stepped in as a saving angel."

Mr. Lin replied that reactionary business people and factory owners might have had such difficulties. " I don't know about that, but as for myself, I have nothing to complain about. I am truly happy that the government has taken over my factories."

He added that he had been interviewed by several other

foreign journalists who had also found it hard to believe that he really meant this. "But what is the use of having a lot of money today?" He waved his plump hands. "One has no use for it—nobody plays mah-jongg any more, or keeps mistresses, or anything like that. We lead a clean and spartan life in new China. I used to have five or six motor cars. Now I have only one—what do I want with more? You cannot eat up the money. I used to be fat and unhealthy, I had a bad heart and could not sleep without pills. Now I have no responsibilities, no worries."

His hand moved down to his belt. "I have lost eighteen pounds since I came back from Hong Kong. Look, my stomach has almost disappeared. I sleep like a log, I . . ."

The telephone rang. Mr. Lin took the call and begged us to excuse him, he had to attend an important meeting.

Outside the door, Chi-yun and I looked at each other. "I can't quite figure him out," I said. "He undoubtedly meant some of what he said, but how much? You are a Chinese—maybe you can tell?"

As an answer, Chi-yun told me an anecdote which she had heard a few days ago. Mao Tse-tung sent for his two second-in-command, Liu Shao-chi and Chou En-lai. "How would you make a cat eat pepper?" he asked them.

"That's easy," replied Liu Shao-chi, the leading Chinese Marxist theorist and a great admirer of Stalin. Many believe that he will succeed Mao. "You get somebody to hold the cat, stuff the pepper into its mouth, and push it down with a chopstick."

"No, no!" Mao raised his hands in horror. "Never use force—that is undemocratic. Everything must be voluntary. How would you do it?" He turned to Chou En-lai.

"I would starve the cat," replied the premier who is more of a diplomat. "Then I would wrap the pepper with a slice of meat. If the cat is sufficiently hungry it will swallow it whole."

Again Mao shook his head. "One must not use deceit either, he said—never fool the people. The two others looked questioningly at him. Then what would he do?

It was so easy, Mao replied—one rubs the pepper thoroughly into the cat's backside. When it begins to burn, the cat will lick it off—and be happy that it is permitted to do so.

" I think Mr. Lin has eaten his pepper," my wife concluded.

CHAPTER XVII

Wei-ti Is Bored

SHORTLY BEFORE THE last war I worked as a reporter on an English-language newspaper in Shanghai. One day I came home and excitedly told my wife that the editor had given me a wonderful assignment.

" I'm going to write a series of articles about prostitution in Shanghai," I said, but then my smile faded. Chi-yun's face clearly showed that she did not share my enthusiasm.

" Why did he have to pick you for that?" she asked. I nearly blurted out the editor's words—" I think this is just the thing for you, Eskelund "—but checked myself in time. We were newly married—perhaps my wife would not appreciate his remark.

During the next two weeks she did not see much of me. " I suppose he is at a brothel," she replied laconically when our friends inquired about me. At first I intended to visit all the houses of ill-fame in Shanghai, but I gave that up when I found out that there were eight hundred registered brothels in the city and many, many more that did not have the blessings of the authorities.

I interviewed girls from all over the world. Most of them were refugees from something—the Bolsheviks, Hitler, famine in the countryside. It was not easy to find a job in crowded Shanghai, so the girls were forced to sell the only thing they had which the metropolis was willing to pay for.

" My parents were in debt," a little Japanese girl told me. They had received 500 Yen for her—about £40 in those days. Her " contract " was for five years. After that she would return to Japan. She blushed as she opened her worn suitcase and took out a photograph.

" This is my fiancé. He is waiting for me."

Such an arrangement is not uncommon in Japan, where people see nothing debasing in prostitution.

A fifteen-year-old Chinese girl offered to share a heroin cigarette with me. She knew that she was ruining her health by smoking, but it made it easier for her to face her job. Once she had been engaged too, but she knew that there was not much chance of her finding a husband now. Not many Chinese will marry a prostitute.

Late one evening I saw a Chinese streetwalker who had found a " customer." I don't think she was more than thirteen or fourteen years old. She took him to a tiny room that opened out to the street. First she went in alone and woke up her family —father, mother, grandmother and four or five little sisters and brothers came out to wait . . .

The girls who worked in brothels were one step higher than the street-walkers. The latter were always accompanied by an elderly woman who acted as a go-between. A girl would lose face if she had to bargain with the customer—even under the most degrading circumstances, the Chinese kept some of their dignity.

There were always prostitutes on the main streets, rows of peasant girls who tried to smile enticingly from under a thick layer of white powder. When the international police made a raid they scattered in all directions. A few would be caught and fined because they had no licence. Before the police-car was out of sight, the girls would be back . . .

" There is no solution to this problem," I said in my last article. But now we were back in Shanghai, and to our amazement we had not seen a single street-walker. We were told that there were no brothels left, either.

How had the Communists succeeded in getting rid of prostitution in the world's fourth or fifth largest city? That was one of the first questions I asked Miss Liu. She should know— though only twenty-five, she was Director of Shanghai's home for the rehabilitation of prostitutes.

We were sitting in the meeting hall which was furnished with rows of wooden benches. On a blackboard were slogans and poems, written by the girls to express their gratitude to Chairman Mao. Through the open window we heard the clacking of machines. The sound came from a nearby building where the girls were working.

As Miss Liu answered my questions she doodled with a pencil. I had a feeling that she was writing an equation. Prostitution = exploitation. Exploitation = sin. How could the authorities prevent people from sinning? By prohibiting it, of course . . .

Shortly after the arrival of the Communists, the brothels were ordered to close down. Most of the owners obeyed; they had a healthy respect for the Communists. The girls were sent back to their homes.

A few of the brothel-owners did not believe that the Communists were in earnest. They tried to continue operating clandestinely. The authorities took care of them.

" What happened to them?"

" They were shot." Miss Liu made a full stop with her pencil. The girls from those brothels had been sent to this home. Some of them were so lethargic from disease and narcotics that everything had to be repeated to them before they understood. One was only twelve years of age.

Some scratched and fought when they were brought in. They had to be held down by force when given injections against venereal diseases. They had never known kindness and could not believe that anybody wanted to help them—most likely their parents had cursed them from the day they were born because they were not boys.

" Before the liberation, life was terrible for many women," Miss Liu said in her gentle voice. My wife nodded. She herself had been given an almost western upbringing. Her parents had both studied in the United States and had a modern outlook. But when she visited her girl friends she had seen how difficult life could be for the women in an old-fashioned Chinese family.

In those days it was common for wealthy men to have several wives. To all appearances it worked quite well. Disagreements were never allowed to come out in the open—the family must not lose face. But the first wife would usually be tortured by jealousy when her husband took a concubine. Then the peace of the home was shattered. The women were always on guard against each other. Who was his favourite? Whose children did he prefer? It always sounded as if the wives spoke politely to each other, but many of their remarks were barbed.

It was the duty of the younger wife to obey the older woman. They would try to load the most unpleasant duties upon her and to humiliate her. The mother-in-law was often very mean. Once she had been badly treated by her husband's mother—now that she had the upper hand, she was going to get her revenge.

When the latest wife lost her husband's affection, a new one would move in. Then she had peace from the others, but no one respected her—not until the other wives were dead and she took over, an embittered old woman ...

" Today, men and women are equal in China," Miss Liu said. " The women have a new dignity ..."

Here I nodded. I remembered what my sister-in-law had said to Chi-yun one of the first days after our arrival. " The Communists have done one thing which we women will always be grateful for. They have taken away our fear—we no longer have to worry over our men fooling around with other women."

Of course all the married men in China have not suddenly lost interest in other women, but they can't get away with it— it is now prohibited to have more than one wife, and there are no prostitutes, so they just have to be good. If a married man starts playing up to a woman, the street committee will soon find out about it. It reports the husband to the Women's League, which sends someone to talk to the sinner. If this warning does not help, a complaint is made to his boss ...

Miss Liu now showed us the rest of the home. In the factory building, more than a hundred girls were standing at their looms. At first glance it looked as if they had grey hair, but it was cotton fluff from the rushing shuttles. The girls looked up, a little glumly, I thought—after all, it is no fun to spend eight hours a day in front of a noisy mechanical monster. But when they discovered that a man had entered, stray locks were quickly pushed in place. They straightened themselves, smiled, and a couple of them flirted so openly that I blushed. The home may have had a good influence upon them, but they did not seem to be entirely cured ...

The dormitories, the kitchen where the girls cooked their own food, the hospital—everything was spick and span. Work was the most important part of the rehabilitation, Miss Liu told us. It gave the girls self-respect. Their wages were twenty per cent lower than at regular factories, but board and lodging, which they had to pay for out of their own pockets, amounted to only about a shilling a day. If they wanted to, they could save nearly five pounds a month.

After work, the girls had two hours of school. About eighty per cent of the 5,000 girls who had been here since the liberation were illiterates, but all could read and write when they left the home. Some spent only six months here, others as much as two years. As soon as they proved that they regretted their old way of life and thought " progressively," they were permitted to leave.

" But who decides whether they have improved sufficiently ?"

" The girls do—they are divided into groups, which make the decision."

" What if the girls make a conspiracy to get each other out ?"

Miss Liu smiled. " My assistants and I also take part in the voting, and of course we would not permit a sister to leave if we thought there was any danger of a relapse. A big city like Shanghai is full of temptations."

When we entered the recreation room, two girls came over to Miss Liu. It was their day off. One of them put her arm around Miss Liu as if she were a schoolmate.

" Our ping-pong ball is broken—may we get a new one."

" Of course." Miss Liu stroked her curly head. The girls may not use make-up, but they are allowed to have permanent waves. " Here is the key to the cupboard."

I began questioning the two girls. The younger one, Wei-ti, was fifteen. Why was she here?

" I was a pickpocket," she repied with a giggle. " At first. I belonged to a gang."

" Were you in need of money?"

" Oh, no." Her family was fairly well off—her father was chief steward on a river steamer, her mother worked at a factory. But there was never anyone at home, and then—well, she had joined this gang.

" Then you were finally caught by the police?"

" No, not for stealing. I was a good pickpocket, I was never caught for that." There was pride in her voice. " But then I began this other thing, and I was caught for that . . ."

Miss Liu explained that Wei-ti had had intimate relations with more than a dozen different men whom she had met through the gang-leader.

" Did they pay you for it?"

" No, never—I didn't even care especially to do it."

" Then why did you?"

She wrinkled her forehead and looked out of the window. Suddenly a smile broke out on her round, childish face.

" Because I was so bored."

Miss Liu said that only a couple of hundred sisters were left at the home. Hardly any of them had been prostitutes. The majority were of Wei-ti's age or slightly older and were guilty of the same offences as she—promiscuity, stealing and hooliganism.

A-feis, the members of these gangs are called. Roughly translated, this means *One who flies.* The name has come about because the boys brush their hair upward in a bold wave.

Were there other ways of recognizing the A-feis? Yes, Wei-ti answered, both the girls and the boys liked to wear tight trousers which they rolled up to just below the knee. They had their own secret slang, and they liked to dance, preferably jazz . . .

" Oh, they're zoot-suiters!" Chi-yun exclaimed.

" It is a new problem," Miss Liu said. A temporary one, she added—she hoped it would disappear by itself when the Communists had carried out all their social reforms . . .

I have heard other Chinese say that these very reforms are

one of the causes of the new delinquency problem. The Communists have done their best to break the power of the older generation over the young. Parents no longer have complete authority over their children. The Shanghai papers recently told about some children who had dragged their father to the police station because he had tried to beat them. He had no right to do so—they were the children of Chairman Mao, the hope of new China.

The former respect for the schoolteacher is also gone. A few months before we came to Shanghai, the papers had carried a story about some High school pupils who beat up their teacher. When the headmaster came he also got a beating. Two policemen who were called to the school fared no better. Finally the chief of police came and tried to reason with the angry youngsters. He was driven away, and a whole squad of policemen armed with truncheons was necessary to quell the riot . . .

Harsh as they are towards poitical offenders, the Communists can be surprisingly lenient with young people. They want very much to win their support and give them as much freedom as possible—but I think they are beginning to discover that freedom is incompatible with Communism.

In Peking I heard of a reformatory for boys many of whom were A-feis. They rioted regularly a couple of times a week, breaking their chopsticks and smashing their ricebowls The teachers were at their wits' end, for they were not supposed to use force, and reason and persuasion just did not work.

About forty per cent of these boys came from " progrcssive " homes. Their fathers were cadres, their mothers had work outside the home. That was as it should be—everybody must work in new China to develop the economy and raise the standard of living.

But the children are left too much to themselves. Even in the evenings they are alone because their parents have to attend meetings. Wei-ti is bored . . .

At noon, all the factories of Shanghai blew their sirens. The gate to the cotton spinnery was thrown open and the girls came streaming out. We rose to leave, but Wei-ti's companion had something to say.

"In a capitalist society, nothing is done for girls like us," she began. "They are trampled down like flowers, but here in the democratic peoples' republic..."

"Oh, stop it!" Wei-ti interrupted. "Keep that for the political meeting tonight—let us go and have lunch."

CHAPTER XVIII

The Will of The People

" DO YOU REMEMBER Wong Heng-li?"

My Chinese friend looked questioningly at me. He had invited me out for dinner; we were through eating and were picking our teeth as people do in China after a meal.

" No, I don't think I know anyone by that name."

" Of course you do! You used to play tennis with him many years ago, he had quite a few foreign friends in those days. They called him Henry . . ."

Henry Wong—oh yes, now I remembered him: a tall, slender Chinese about my own age. He had many gold fillings in his front teeth—they would glisten in the sun when he smiled shyly across the tennis net. He was apologetic because he always won. Sometimes he would try to lose, but he seldom succeeded . . .

" He wants very much to see you," my friend continued, but he shook his head when I suggested that Henry could come and visit me at the hotel.

" He can't get in at the hotel without giving his name and address to the portier. Henry has had a lot of trouble with the authorities—it would be better if they didn't know about it. Can't you look him up?"

" But then his neighbours will see me and report it."

" He has no neighbours. He lives in a little house just outside the town. He is practically always at home . . ."

The next morning I went out to see Henry. I took a bus to the last stop and then walked. Soon I had passed the last houses and was in the country. The air was clear and fresh and it was wonderfully quiet after the noises of the city.

I came to a small farmhouse. The paper windows were

hinese
atching the
rvice at a
ama temple
Peking,
stored at
vernment
pense and
own to all
sitors—look,
ere is freedom
religion in
w China.

a Shanghai
mple—the
retaker's
mily have
nch.

Peking now has four hostels for farmers who come to the city. Here two are playing dominoes in the dormitory.

Like a glimpse of the old, unhurried days.

inese farmer
they often go
nting to
rn an extra
nny—it is
rd to make
th ends meet
ese days.

n a collective
rm in
orth China.

She has learnt
to handle
the chopsticks
but it is
easier when
"ma" helps
out—in North
China this is
the usual word
for mother.

The
Sanmen Gorge
on the
Yellow River.

broken and you could see the bamboo skeleton where the clay had been washed off the wall by the rain. He cannot be living here, I thought, but just then a tall, stooping man appeared in the door.

"Hello, Karl!" I remembered him as a smartly-dressed young man in a European suit. Now he wore blue cotton clothes, crumpled and not very clean. He shook my hand and slapped me on the shoulder. The gold fillings glistened.

"I'll make a cup of tea," he said. He talked incessantly of the old days as he struggled to light a primus. There was something hectic in his manner as if he feared that time was running short.

I looked about me in the little room. Dust had gathered in the spiders' webs underneath the eaves. There was a camp bed, two chairs and a battered writing desk. On a stack of books stood a silver shield. The metal was so tarnished that I had to hold it up to read the inscription: "First Prize in Men's Singles, August, 1941."

The primus finally began to hiss. Henry sat down on the camp bed. "You have no idea how happy I am to see you! It is so seldom I can talk to anyone. Are you in a hurry?"

He looked anxiously at me. I had only planned to stay for a while, but shook my head. Henry smiled relieved and went on talking. Did I remember Jack, the left-handed player? And Heinrich, the melancholy German? And that evening when we went dancing...

The water began to boil. When Henry had poured the tea he sat down with his hands clasped arounnd one knee. "I read in the papers that you are going to write a book about China. How long have you been here?"

"Three months."

"And what do you think of new China?"

I hesitated. It was hard to explain my own feelings; they were so mixed up.

"One moment I am full of enthusiasm for everything the Communists have done—the beggars have disappeared, the workers are better off, there is no more corruption, and the

L

industrial progress is incredible. But the next moment I think that too high a price has been paid for this progress. China has been put in a straight-jacket of fear—nobody speaks freely any more, people hardly dare to think. No place has ever depressed me so much—though I suppose that people coming from western Europe are bound to feel that way. I am longing to get away, and so is my wife."

Henry nodded. " As a foreigner, it must be difficult for you to find out what is really going on."

" Yes—not because the Communists have put any obstacles in my way. I can travel freely, it is easy enough to get permission if you only apply in time. I can talk to anyone I want to, but even so I have a feeling that I see only one side of the picture. People I interview always say the same thing—all I hear is praise . . ."

" What do you expect?" Henry interrupted. " You see only the side which the Communists want to show you—the same side they show to all the foreign delegations that come for a short visit."

He told me that one of his friends had belonged to a group that entertained a foreign delegation. " First they had a rehearsal. They tried to imagine what the foreign guests would ask and then worked out suitable answers. And of course the whole group was made up of people who were thought to be friendly towards the government."

" Are there many who don't like the government?"

Henry shrugged. " I don't know. Those who have something to say against the government keep their mouths shut. Nobody discusses politics except at the regular political meetings. I might get into trouble for talking to you, but I want you to know what is going on—there is so much deceit and hypocrisy, it is enough to make you sick!" He spat on the earthen floor. " And if you write about it, be sure to do it in such a way that they won't know whom you got it from. You must promise me that, Karl!"

" Yes, of course."

" You know, the funny thing is that I don't really have very much against the Communists. In many ways I admire them.

Most of what they have done was necessary for China. The old society was so rotten . . ."

He had been a sworn enemy of Chiang Kai-shek. I remembered from our tennis games how he had sometimes swung his racket violently, making me expect a fast shot. Instead came a soft ball that just dropped over the net so I had no chance of reaching it. Then he would grin and say: " That was a cheater—a Chiang Kai-shek!"

" I was glad when the Communists came," he continued. " I could easily have gone to Hong Kong, but I preferred to stay. Not that I am very idealistic, but I wanted to take part in the rebuilding of China."

At that time Henry had an American business partner. They imported canned goods and toilet articles, mainly from the U.S.A. When the Communists approached the city, the American left and Henry took over the firm. He had good business just after the liberation. Imports had practically come to a standstill, but he had large stocks to sell from.

One day he was called to a political meeting. Among those present were several businessmen whom he knew. A Communist official lectured them on the duties of patriotic business people. He attacked the Americans, calling them terrible names. The Chinese do not like to hear such rantings, they find it undignified, but the businessmen listened impassively—they were already used to the vituperations of the Communists. You read it in the papers and heard it on the radio every day.

When the lecture was over, they clapped dutifully and rose to leave.

" One moment." The Communist asked them to sit down again. " Some of those present have formerly co-operated with the Americans."

He looked at Henry. " As far as I understand, you used to have an American partner. Is that correct?"

" Yes."

" Please tell us about the crimes which this American committed against the Chinese people." He explained that a campaign would soon be started to expose the criminal activities of the foreign business people. The people must be made to realize that they had been deceived and exploited not only by the Chiang Kai-shek government, but also by the foreign imperialists. Comrade Wong could begin with an exposé of his former partner . . .

"But he did not do anything wrong," Henry protested. "He was an honest and decent businessman."

The Communist smiled ironically. "He was an American Imperialist and therefore an enemy of the people. I advise you to tell us everything you know about his reactionary activities. That will make it easier for you when we start looking into your own past. There will be another meeting the day after tomorrow. By then we expect a truthful report from you."

The businessmen were also told to attend a mass meeting which would take place in a park on the following afternon. It was the first of the big public trials in which the Communists squared up accounts with the past.

"The place was swarming with people," Henry told me. The street committees had been told to make sure that everyone from the district attended. Flags fluttered, the loudspeakers blared one march after another, and the fruit and candy vendors did a roaring business. The whole thing reminded one of the yearly spring festival.

Then a couple of hundred people with their hands tied to their backs were led to a platform. They stood with bowed heads while the mayor denounced them. His speech lasted for two hours . . .

Henry rose and went over to his desk. "I still have a newspaper report of the proceedings. Here it is." He took out a clipping and translated it for me.

" . . . for each word, the bitter hatred of the people was blown more white-hot. Finally the mayor pointed at the prisoners and said : ' comrades, what shall we do with all these criminals, bandits, secret agents, evil landlords, and heads and organizers of reactionary religious sects?' ' Shoot them !' roared the people in one voice . . . 'We are here representing the people,' the mayor said. ' It is our duty to do the will of the people. Let the people's sentence be carried out . . .' "

Henry looked at me for a moment. He folded the clipping and put it away. Then he continued.

At the meeting with the business people the following day, the Communist came straight to the point. Would Comrade Wong, as a patriotic Chinese, reveal the crimes of his former American partner? Or did he choose to side with the reactionary enemies of the people?

" I will gladly tell everything I know," Henry replied. " But how can I accuse him of something which he has not done?"

" As you wish. Perhaps there are others present who prefer to take a more positive attitude?"

There were. Several of the businessmen had brought along written accusations against their former foreign business associates. They were read aloud. The accusations rang out in the meeting hall—corruption, cheating, collaboration with Chiang Kai-shek agents, theft of state secrets, espionage . . .

The next morning, Henry saw his own picture on the front pages of all the newspapers. " Big tiger exposed," the captions said. That was the term used for people who had exploited the masses—they had the greed and cunning of the tiger.

The papers said that Henry had been the accomplice of an American who had swindled the Chinese people out of huge sums. Of course the " big tiger " had attempted to hide his sinful past, but the authorities were now gathering evidence against him. In addition to everything else, it was suspected that he and his American partners had been agents of an imperialistic foreign power.

When Henry turned on the radio he heard the same story. At the office he could immediately sense a change in his subordinates. They all avoided looking at him. On his desk he found a resolution, signed by the whole staff : " We must condemn your unpatriotic attitude . . . The enemies of the people are our enemies . . . The truth cannot be hidden from the people . . . We advise you to confess everything . . ."

Henry usually lunched with a couple of business friends at a nearby restaurant. That day they did not come. Everyone stopped talking when he entered the restaurant. People whispered and looked at him covertly. The waiter, who usually joked with him, seemed to be on the edge of tears. When he brought the food, he whispered that he had read about Henry's case. " I am sorry for you. Better confess . . ."

In the afternoon, a delegation of businessmen came to Henry's office. They advised him strongly to co-operate with the authorities. Henry repeated that he wanted to, but he could not say something that was not true.

" But one does not have to have proofs," one of the business-men said. " It is enough if you only have a suspicion. Just write that your former partner probably did many bad things behind your back. They will be satisfied with that. Times have changed —we have to change too. And after all it cannot do any harm to him, he is out of the country already."

Henry replied that he could not do it. When they were gone he sat alone in his office. He could not work. His thoughts kept returning to the mass meeting in the park.

His wife was not at home when he came back. The telephone rang. It was the Communist official. No use to keep anything back now, he said—Henry's wife had gone to the police and confessed everything. It was Henry's last chance to confess . . .

" I sat for a long while with the receiver in my hand," Henry told me. " I was shocked and frightened, but still I could not do what they wanted me to."

" Was it true what he said about your wife ?"

" I'm not sure. She had come under the influence of some progressive friends who had convinced her that I was a bad man—a capitalist and exploiter and all that. She left me. Later she wrote that she did not want to live with me any more because I defended an American Imperialist. We were divorced."

In the evening the street committee sent for him. A special meeting had been called to discuss his case. Henry was placed in the centre of the room. Then his neighbours began to make accusations against him. He had often had foreign visitors. Late one night, people had seen him and his American friend carry mysterious boxes into the apartment. What was in those boxes ? Was it something that the servants were not supposed to know about ?

" It was some boxes of whisky which my partner once got me at a cheap price," Henry told me. " But nobody would believe that. They insisted that it was a radio sender and secret documents. I told them that they were welcome to search my apartment, but they didn't want to do that. Of course I had already removed all the traces, they said—I was a cunning, dangerous enemy."

In the end they elected a four-man committee to look into Henry's past. The committee was composed of one Communist and three " progressives." During the next two weeks Henry had no peace. The grilling began every afternoon and sometimes lasted until late at night. He had to tell everything he could remember about his past, and they kept trying to trap him.

" The Communist wasn't so bad," Henry said. " He was polite—dogmatic, of course, but otherwise quite sensible. The progressives were unbearable. They were out to prove how patriotic they were. Everything I said was twisted around and turned against me. It was useless to argue with them. I was often infuriated, but of course I had to control myself."

In the mornings he had to be at his office and go through the books with a young Communist official. " He was twenty-two. He knew a lot of Marxism, but nothing about business. Every time there was an entry about a commission, he took it for bribery. He got terribly excited when he discovered that my former partner had taken 50,000 American dollars with him when he left. I explained that it had not been unlawful at the time, but he insisted that it was *morally* wrong, I should have known that, the money represented the sweat and blood of the Chinese people. I was the American's accomplice . . ."

The young Communist also said that it was shameless of Henry to have chosen such a profession. He could not have a good character, or he would have preferred to do something for the people, something constructive, instead of becoming a business man . . .

The business life of the city had come to a standstill during this period. Tens of thousands were accused of corruption. People were urged to inform the authorities if they suspected anyone. At all offices and in public buildings were special boxes for letters informing on people. It was made clear that those who assisted the authorities by giving information about others would be leniently treated if there were any misdemeanours in their own past.

The Communists tried to make it look as if they were not behind this movement. "That is an obsession with them," Henry told me. "They always leave the dirty work to the committees and the progressives. Then they step back and say : it is the will of the people."

Almost every day there were public trials in the parks. These trials were broadcast over the radio and relayed by public loudspeakers—you could hear the shrill shouts of the prosecutor all over the city : enemy of the people, traitor ! Then came the roar of the crowd : kill, kill ! In between you could hear the sirens of the ambulances. Day and night they were busy removing the bodies of those who could not take it and had committed suicide.

"I don't know how many took their own lives, there was never a word about it in the papers, but it must have been thousands. People didn't dare use the sidewalks—you never knew when someone would jump out of a window. One morning on my way to the office I passed three crowds which had gathered around the bodies of people who had just bumped."

Henry got up and paced the floor. "It was a nightmare. And it was not the guilty ones who took their own lives. It was those who were too sensitive to stand the pressure. I knew a nurse, an honest, conscientious girl. She was asked to say if she had done anything wrong in her past. Yes, she replied, once a foreign patient at the hospital where she worked had forgotten a couple of dollars in a drawer. She tried to get in touch with the patient, but he had left China. What had become of the money ? She had just kept it, what else could she do ?

"They said she was a common thief. If she had been able to do such a thing, she must have other crimes on her conscience. She wept and assured them that there was nothing else, but they would not believe her—she had better confess, they said. Finally she jumped out from the third floor."

Everyone was told to write his life history. " I don't remember how many times I had to do it," Henry said. " It was rejected time and again. I wasn't straightforward, I had an anti-social attitude, I had not confessed everything. Everybody knew that the Communists weren't satisfied until you had confessed something or other. People would ask each other : What shall I confess? Many invented small offences so they wouldn't have to keep on re-writing their histories."

The street committees were untiring in organizing political meetings. Everybody had to join. A well-known businessman marched at the head of a procession, carrying a red flag and shouting patriotic slogans. Then he went home and shot himself.

When the public trials had been going on for a couple of weeks, Henry was arrested. " They put me in a dark cell with about fifty other people. We slept on the floor. The food was terrible and the place was full of vermin, but worst of all, there was no toilet. Every morning and evening they would bring a pail, one minute for each, a guard would time us. But even so I preferred the prison—at least I was left in peace by the damned progressives who had pestered me when I was free !"

Almost every morning, some prisoners would be led away to the public trials. They did not return, but their places were quickly taken by others—all educated people.

Henry was questioned a couple of times a week. " I did not hide anything from them, but it was very difficult to convince them of that. I was a capitalist, an exploiter of the people, and on top of that I was obstinate—there just *had* to be something on my conscience. But it was impossible for them to find any inconsistencies in what I had said, and my firm's books were in perfect order. They were amazed when they finally realized that I had not tried to deceive them. Then they let me out."

By then he had been locked up for over five months. They did not acknowledge their mistake in arresting him.

Soon after this he had to liquidate his business. All commerce was now controlled by the State, and as he was still considered a reactionary he was given no contracts. Most of the money which he realized from the liquidation went for paying taxes and fines.

" I still have a little left, though—enough to manage for a year or two. As you see, I live rather modestly now."

" What will you do when your money runs out?"

" Then I will have to take a job. It isn't hard for people with my education to get something to do, but . . ." He sat down again. How tired he looked. " But first I will have to change myself, and that isn't easy. I have to learn to think differently. Otherwise nobody will give me a job . . ."

The Communists had classified him as a " reactionary intellectual." Three times a week he went to meetings with about twenty others who were going through the same re-education course. " Of course the leader of our group is a progressive. We analyse the news. He doesn't say much—he just sits there and listens and takes down every word. But I can always tell from his face when I say something wrong—that is, from his point of view. And I do practically every time I open my big mouth. It is not enough just to say that you agree with the Government. You have to prove that the Communists always do the right thing, that they always think of the welfare of the people. As long as you have any doubts about this, you will not be approved by the progressive group leader. I have been going to those meetings for nearly three years. I'm afraid I haven't improved much."

Every new campaign was discussed at the meetings. There was always a new campaign—against counter-revolutionaries, bureaucracy, waste; against the sparrows which ate too much of the grain of The People's Republic. For a while whole families would go sparrow-hunting on Sundays, it was the patriotic thing to do. One campaign was directed against harmful insects. Afterwards the government announced that 18,500 billion flies and mosquitoes had been liquidated, mostly by handpower. Throughout the country the children had been given flyswatters . . .

" There has also been a campaign against too many campaigns," Henry continued. " And at the moment there is a campaign to make people express themselves freely."

" Yes, I've heard about that."

" There are some who dare to criticize a little—you have probably read some of the letters to the editor in the newspapers. The toothpaste tubes are no good and the radiators in the new workers' dwellings leak and so on. But the real problems that we have inside of us—nobody dares to talk about them. Not even with your best friend. You never know whom you can trust any more."

" Can't you leave ?"

" What do you mean ?"

" Leave China—go to Hong Kong."

He shook his head. " First of all, I can't get permission to leave the country. And even if I did succeed in getting to Hong Kong, the people there would suspect me of being a Communist agent. No, Karl, I have to stay. I have to learn to *think constructively,* as they call it. And I suppose I can— maybe it will be easier for me when I have no more to eat."

We talked on for a while. When I left he accompanied me part of the way. When we were approaching the first house, he stopped and held out his hand.

" Goodbye, Karl. Thanks for coming."

" Goodbye . . ." I wanted so much to leave him a word of encouragement, but what could I say ? " Good luck," I added lamely. Then we parted.

INDEX